100 THAI WORDS TO START

SPEAKING
THAI

ISBN 978-1-912145-28-7

ARUN
PRESS

ACKNOWLEDGEMENTS

I would like to thank the following people for their help and support, without whom completing this book would not be possible:

- **Bangorn Maneekong** – for all her help and advice with writing the Thai script and for being my wife!
- **Anonglak Songprakone** – for her proofreading of the book.
- **Ali Dewji** – for his consistently helpful and positive support in the design and production of the book.

CONTENTS

See the back of the book for the full list of 100 words listed by the English word and meaning for easy lookup.

PREFACE

- Do you want to say a few simple words and sentences in Thai to make your experience of Thailand even more memorable?

- Are you after a simple handbook that gives you the most relevant and common basic words and example sentences?

- Do you prefer a guide to a textbook? Do you want some insight to help you know when to use which word and why?

If you answered "Yes", this book is for you.

Thailand is a truly special place and hopefully you will, or already have fallen in love with the country, the people and way of life.

Making even the smallest effort to speak Thai is very much appreciated by Thai people. I can still remember my first, slightly nervous attempts to speak a few words of Thai more than fifteen years ago and their and my mutual thrill when I got it right and was understood.

Looking back, I still smile at how I mispronounced or misunderstood but those first interactions are still some of my fondest memories of Thailand.

I hope this book helps you to leave Thailand with similarly long lasting fond memories or perhaps, convince you to visit again or even move to Thailand for a longer period.

When I learnt Thai, there was no book like this so I wrote this book for those of you who are just like I was then – keen to make a good impression as a visitor to Thailand and wanting to establish some sort of connection with the people beyond just a foreign tourist or customer context and feel the warmth and thrill of being able to engage with Thai people in their own language.

What makes this book different?

- **Combination of a phrasebook and a textbook:** while phrasebooks are useful to look up and copy sentences, they can be limited – often the sentence doesn't match your exact situation and do you want to look up your book every single time you try to speak to someone? Conversely, textbooks teach you basic Thai but do you really want to study Thai? This book combines the best aspects of both – you get the words you need and example sentences and not the ones you will never use. There are also no roleplay exercises or tests at the end of the chapter – hope you agree.

- **'Blog' style:** written in a style that is actually helpful to you, as if I am speaking to you. No stuffy instructions and grammar dictated to you but still giving you the Thai you need.

- **Proper grouping of words:** grouping of words in a way that allows easy reference for common situations but also grouping according to types of words e.g. verbs and adjectives. This is far more useful when you want to use a word to fit your own situation rather than waiting for a chance to recite the one phrase you have memorised.

- **Tips and insight:** possibly the biggest differentiator to most books out there, the tips and insight in this book tell you when to use words, in what context and why.

- **Words omitted from this book:** another big differentiator is the words I have left out of this book e.g. telling the time or colours. Why? One reason is telling the time is quite tricky in Thai and you are unlikely to need to do it in Thai anyway. Similarly, colours are a bit unnecessary because you can and probably will just point and are unlikely to be having a conversation with a seller in Thai that would lead to having to say a colour in Thai. Right? Throughout this book I have recognised that as a newcomer to Thai, you will spend most of your time speaking in English to locals and you are not looking for a coursebook in basic Thai. So you get the words and sentences that will be most useful and will make the best impression with the least effort needed to learn Thai. Agreed?

- **Size:** and finally, the book is sized to be a handy companion.

ABOUT THE AUTHOR

I first went to Thailand on a business trip and, like many people, absolutely loved it. From the food, to the people, the sights and smells, the lifestyle, the natural beauty, to the nightlife...basically I could not wait to go back.

I went back a couple more times for a holiday by which time I had already begun learning Thai in London at home using a couple of books. I then was offered to relocate to Thailand for work and that is where my progress in speaking (and reading) Thai increased rapidly. After a few years, I married a Thai colleague and moved back to London to continue our banking careers.

Over ten years on from back then, and after numerous trips to Thailand for holidays and to see family, I have moved from London back to Thailand all over again.

Now I spend more time writing books on Thai where I see a gap in the quality of books out there. So, in the beginners' area, I noticed there are lots of books that are more textbook-like that will not appeal to people who do not necessarily want to learn Thai in any depth. Conversely, there are also lots of books that are phrasebooks without much explanation of context or insight, which makes all the difference to learning. While phrasebooks are certainly useful, with a tonal language such as Thai, where pronunciation is key, trying to recite a Thai phrase – written in English – out of a book is an exercise doomed to failure and leading to blank, confused looks and misunderstanddings. I hope you agree and enjoy the book – written in recognition that you want to enjoy your trip, not study Thai the whole time.

TRANSLITERATION AND GUIDE TO PRONUNCIATION

This book, written at a beginner level, does not go into all the grammar rules of Thai. Therefore, the below section is what I believe is the minimum guidance you need to be able to read this book and reproduce the sounds reasonably accurately. I have assumed you do not want an extensive chapter on all the pronunciation rules and structures but just want to get up to speed as quickly as possible.

(For those that do want to study Thai at basic level, which I define as next after beginner, check out **James Higbie**'s excellent book – **Essential Thai**, including a comprehensive guide to transliteration and pronunciation.) Also, I do not want to put you off learning Thai by giving you a huge breakdown of all the pronunciation rules.

Conversely, do remember that Thai is tonal language so getting the tone wrong doesn't just mean you mispronounced, it often means you said a completely different word. However, as long as you realize pronunciation is important in a tonal language, don't let it stop you. Yes, you will mispronounce a lot initially but you may still be understood from the context and you are far better off trying, failing and then asking where you mispronounced than spending forever fretting about making mistakes and never experiencing the joy of engaging with Thai people in their own language.

Tones and vowel length
Long syllables have no '_' while short syllables will always have an '_' underneath. Double vowels indicate longer sounds if there is no '_'. Therefore, 'tóok' is a shorter, more stunted sound; even though it is a double vowel, the underline always takes

precedence and shortens the sound. Conversely, 'bprà-têt' only has a single 'e' but is a longer 'e' sound like *'get'* but holding the 'e' for longer – "*geeet outta my way*". Hyphenated words are to show the syllable breakdown, not a spoken pause.

There are five tones in Thai – medium or monotone, lòw, hígh, rǐsing (like "oh yeeaah??") and fâlling ("oh nooo!!").

Consonants

Dt – this is a sound between a 'd' and 't' i.e. a soft 't', like *'style'* but softer with the tip of the tongue under the front teeth, which is different to both *'day'* and *'table'*.

Bp – this is a sound between a 'b' and 'p', like *'suppose'*, which is different to *'bread'* and *'party'*.

The other consonants are largely the same sound as in English. There are some subtle differences in aspiration and sound hardness but you can absorb these as you interact with Thai people. The one that I will mention for now is the 'k' in words starting with 'k' in Thai is a rougher sound than in English – more like a 'kh'.

Vowels

There are short and long versions of most vowels. I have not listed every single one of these because in most cases, the double vowelled transliteration will make it obvious and, as discussed above, the underlines always take precedence and are the definitive indicator of short sounds.

A – as in '*Obama*', NOT '*cat*'

Ae – as in the first and third 'a' in '*caravan*'

O – as in '*go*', NOT '*pot*'; longer version spelt with an h – '*mohng*'

Aw – as in '*Squawk*' (slight American accent to bring the lower jaw down)

Ooy – as in *'loiter'* (posh English accent) but a bit elongated, rounded 'o'

U – as in '*fun*', NOT '*rude*' when it is a 'u' by itself; when it is part of a combination vowel such as 'ua', 'ui' or 'uay', it is 'u' as in '*rude*'.

Eu – as in "*err...what do you mean?*"

Oi – as in 'Aw' above with a 'y' sound at the end; 'Ooi' is more elongated

~~Eu~~ – no real equivalent in English but the closest is '*dude*' (like in all the LA teen films) said with a smile and the mouth stretched out. Elongated sound.

There are many more vowels and vowel combinations but I am hoping most of these should be obvious from the transliteration and if not, do reference the plethora of material on this topic online and in books. So for example, I hope when you see 'tîao', you will be able to pronounce this based on my explanation of the falling tone earlier in this chapter and using common sense to work out how an 'iao' sound would sound. So I have left it to you to work out these vowel combinations rather than list them all here. Ok?

Finally, a quick note that there are a few words that are pronounced slightly differently in spoken Thai compared to written Thai. I have chosen to use the spoken language spelling in the transliterated Thai for these few words. 'sa-baai', 'chún' and 'a-ròi' are examples of these. The difference is slight so don't stress about it. I have also highlighted one or two words where the 'r' sound is more like 'l', as is common in Asia.

1. ABSOLUTE BASICS / GREETINGS

Words covered in this chapter

sa-wat-dee	สวัสดี	hello
krup / ka	ครับ / ค่ะ / คะ	politeness particle
kawp koon	ขอบคุณ	thank you
mai bpen rai	ไม่เป็นไร	never mind / it's ok
dee / mai dee	ดี / ไม่ดี	good / bad
chai / mai / mai chai	ใช่ / ไม่ / ไม่ใช่	yes / no / not true **
sa-baai dee	สบายดี	(to be) well / fine
kaw-toht	ขอโทษ	sorry
pom (m) / chun (f) / kao	ผม / ฉัน / เขา	I (pom / chun) / he / she (kao)
chohk dee	โชคดี	good luck

NB: Transliteration above and below written without tone or other pronunciation marks.

** Note that, in Thai, there is no single word that means 'yes' in all contexts in Thai! Pay special attention to the explanation of this word 6 because 'chai' more accurately means 'that's right' or 'correct' so it can be used to mean 'yes' when the question is 'it's hot isn't it?' but NOT when the question is 'are you hungry?' because using 'chai' would mean saying 'that's right' in response and makes no sense in Thai…or English.

21

Tips / in my experience / insight: *before we begin, I want to highlight a key cultural point relevant to greetings. – the 'wâai' i.e. the familiar palms together gesture. Generally, as a foreigner, you should NOT 'wâai' first as you will probably not be in a situation that requires it. Don't initiate a 'wâai' to shop staff or younger people or taxi drivers etc. It is not really the right thing to do – notice no Thai person ever 'wâai's shop staff first.*

Generally speaking, the person with seniority, whether by age, social or situational status 'wâai's the other first, so customers are shown respect by getting 'wâai''d first by staff. A polite mini-head bow or nod in response is fine but you can, by all means, 'wâai' back if you want. You should, however, definitely 'wâai' your girlfriend's mother and do it right – do NOT flare out your elbows like a martial artist! NB: see fuller explanation at the back.

1. <u>sa</u>-<u>wàt</u> dee สวัสดี

Meaning – hello (and goodbye)

Context – obviously the first word to learn and almost always followed by the next word – '<u>krúp</u> / <u>kà</u>'.

Example:

<u>Sa</u>-<u>wàt</u> dee <u>krúp</u> / <u>Sa</u>-<u>wàt</u> dee <u>kà</u>.

สวัสดีครับ / สวัสดีค่ะ

Hello.

Men use the '<u>krúp</u>' ending; women use '<u>kà</u>' for statements and '<u>ká</u>' for questions. (Btw, the reason you see 'sawasdee' written with an 's' is that that is how it is spelt in Thai but the 's' converts to a 't' sound when spoken.)

Tips / in my experience / insight: *so what insight could there be for as simple a word as 'hello'? Well, for starters, you will hear two different versions from women – 'sa-wàt dee kà' is the standard one but you will also hear the falling tone ending, which is often used when 'hello' is said as a response or just for more emphasis or humility / politeness / warmth / familiarity. For example, you will often hear shop assistants at the mall or TV presenters say closer to 'kâ'. And often, when the speaker is in a service role or the host, it is elongated with extra 'a's – 'kâaa' - leave this version to Thais while you're a beginner.*

Second, note that Thai people do not formally say 'sa-wàt dee' as much as Westerners. You will hear it being said more often in formal and semi-formal settings (such as customer / seller) and where politeness is important.

Third, as a foreigner in Thailand, you should default to being more polite and formal where in doubt. So, yes, you may say '_sa-wàt dee krúp_' more often than people around you (as you will notice when two Thai people walk up to each other or meet up and do not necessarily start off with 'hello') but don't let that worry you. It is clearly correct to say 'hello'!

Fourth, '_wàt dee_' is a short version for close friends so not appropriate for you as a tourist.

Finally, '_sa-wàt dee_' is used for 'goodbye' too. Just as with 'hello', 'goodbye' is not formally said in many everyday situations but you will often hear it at the end of phone conversations (e.g. on TV or on the Skytrain) and you are perfectly entitled to use it yourself. As you get more familiar with Thai, you will hear several less formal ways of saying 'goodbye', including saying nothing in particular.

2. <u>krúp</u> / <u>kà</u> / <u>ká</u> ครับ / ค่ะ / คะ

Meaning – politeness particle

Context – possibly the most common word in Thai, in its main usage, is added to the end of sentences and questions. It has no meaning of its own but adds politeness and formality to statements, responses and questions.

Politeness, especially with people who you do not know, older or more senior people or where it is a formal / semi-formal situation is absolutely critical so this particle will be added to almost every sentence by a shopkeeper to a customer, for example.

Tips / in my experience / insight: *as mentioned previously, you will hear variations in the tone of this word. 'krúp' (colloquially, 'khúp)' is sometimes slightly elongated for a bit more emphasis and similarly, 'kà' is often elongated and changed to a falling tone 'kâaa' for more feeling when responding.*

Not too different to English where we elongate words for more emphasis. You should just stick to the standard 'krúp' / 'kà'.

For questions, as you would expect, it is 'ká' with a high tone.

A more subtle use of 'krúp / kà' is as a simple substitute for 'yes' or 'ok'. So you may hear conversations where one party is only saying this word in response; this is similar to saying "yep, yeah, ok, sure...".

3. kàwp <u>koon</u> ขอบคุณ

Meaning – thank you

Context – fairly straightforward word albeit there are several other less formal ways to say *'thank you'*, just as there are in English.

Example:
Kàwp <u>koon</u> <u>krúp</u> / <u>kà</u>.

ขอบคุณครับ / ค่ะ

Thank you.

A reminder that the 'k' in Thai is a rougher sound, almost a 'kh'. Indeed, you will some people use quite a throaty 'kh' so feel free to go with the speaking style you like best.

4. <u>mâi bpen rai</u> ไม่เป็นไร

Meaning – never mind / it's ok

Context – used very commonly and in the same way as in English.

Example:
Person A: Kàwp <u>koon</u> <u>krúp</u>. Person B: <u>Mâi bpen rai</u> <u>kà</u>.

คนแรก: ขอบคุณครับ คนที่สอง: ไม่เป็นไรค่ะ

Person A: Thank you. Person B: It's nothing (more literally) / no problem / no worries / don't mention it etc.

Often the response will just be 'kâ' for short (if it is a woman responding obviously).

5. dee / <u>mâi</u> dee ดี / ไม่ดี

Meaning – good / not good

Context – already mentioned in word no. 1, this is an easy word to learn and pronounce due to being mid tone. And, as in the example below, a very useful word for short responses or statements of opinion.

Example:
Person A: <u>Bpai</u> '<u>cháwp</u>-<u>bpîng</u>' <u>gun</u> dee <u>mái</u> <u>ká</u>? Person B: Dee <u>krúp</u>.

คนแรก: ไปชอปปิ้งกันดีไหมคะ คนที่สอง: ดีครับ

Person A: Want to go shopping? Person B: Sure. (using 'good' as a response – something like "sure, good idea").

Tips / in my experience / insight: *just knowing this word – 'dee' – can allow you to respond to simple questions and indicate your willingness to speak Thai (which is always appreciated).*

Moreover, to make your first tentative attempts to speak Thai, you should try to use this word to respond simply in Thai to suggestions such as the above even if they are asked in English (which is obviously a lot more likely, given that the Thai person you are with will know you are new to Thai). This small simple attempt to respond in Thai will be appreciated and is exactly the kind of thing I did on my first trip.

And, if, like I did, you want to show a bit of enthusiasm or intentionally be a bit over the top to break the ice, you can add on word no. 12 to 'dee'. Try it out for yourself.

6. __châi__ / __mâi__ / __mâi châi__ ใช่ / ไม่ / ไม่ใช่

Meaning – yes / no / not (true)

Context – *'yes'* and *'no'* do not have direct equivalents in Thai in every context – the context is key. While you can, in some usages, respond to questions with just *'yes'* or *'no'* in Thai (as shown in the example sentences), in MOST situations, you CANNOT. The reason is '__châi__', strictly speaking, means *'(that is) true'* and '__mâi châi__' accurately means *'not true'*. So if the question needs a confirmation, the Thai usage effectively means *'yes'* as in English.

For any questions with an adjective or a verb, a correct response needs to __repeat the__

<u>adjective or verb</u>. So, for example, in English, if someone asks, *"Is it cold?"*, you could simply answer *"yes"* or *"no"*, albeit it would sound abrupt if you did not say anything else at all in response. In Thai, you need to repeat the adjective, as shown below. If you have been to Singapore, you should be familiar with this style of response...remember *"can, can"* or even *"cannot"*? Sounds odd to native English speakers but is logical and succinct.

Example:

Person A: Châwp <u>mái</u> <u>krúp</u>? Person B: <u>Mâi</u> châwp <u>krúp</u>.

คนแรก: ชอบไหมครับ คนที่สอง: ไม่ชอบครับ

Person A: Do you like it? Person B: No (I don't). (Literally, 'not like').

Note that if the answer was to be *'yes'*, you would simply say "Châwp <u>krúp</u>".

Person A: <u>Bpai</u> tîao <u>mái</u> <u>ká</u>? Person B: <u>Bpai</u> <u>krúp</u>.

คนแรก: ไปเที่ยวไหมคะ คนที่สอง: ไปครับ

Person A: Want to go out / travelling? Person B: Yeah, sure.

As you can see, to answer *'yes'* you need to just repeat the verb, NOT '<u>châi</u>'.

Person A: Koon maa jàak <u>À</u>-me-<u>rí</u>-gaa <u>châi</u> <u>mái</u>? Person B: <u>Châi</u> <u>krúp</u>.

คนแรก: คุณมาจากอเมริกาใช่ไหม คนที่สอง: ใช่ครับ

Person A: You're from America, right? Person B: Yeah (that's right) / Yes, I am.

So, as mentioned before, '<u>châi</u>' by itself means more like *'yes, that's true'* so it is usually used when agreeing with someone's statement or opinion or confirming.

Person A: Doo năng sa-nòok mái ká? Person B: Sa-nòok krúp.

คนแรก: ดูหนังสนุกไหมคะ คนที่สอง: สนุกครับ

Person A: Was the film good? Person B: Yeah.

Person A: Bpai gùp faen rĕuh? Person B: Mâi châi krúp. Bpai gùp pêuan.

คนแรก: ไปกับแฟนเหรอ   คนที่สอง: ไม่ใช่ครับ ไปกับเพื่อน

Person A: Did you go with your girlfriend? Person B: No (literally – 'not true'), I went with a friend / friends.

Notice that the past tense above still uses 'bpai', because it is obvious from the question that we are talking about the past so there is no need for verb conjugation. Also notice Thai does not specify plurals: 'pêuan'.

7. <u>sa</u>-baai dee สบายดี

Meaning – to be well / fine

Context – the concept of being '<u>sa</u>-baai' is one of the absolutely central to Thai lifestyle. It means *'to be comfortable'* or *'nice and easy'* etc. (so no surprise so many massage parlours are called 'Sabai' or similar. In the usage below, it is literally *'well and good'*.

Example:

Person A: <u>Sa</u>-baai dee <u>mái</u> <u>ká</u>? Person B: <u>Sa</u>-baai dee <u>krúp</u>.

คนแรก: สบายดีไหมคะ คนที่สอง: สบายดีครับ

Person A: How are you? Person B: I'm fine / well.

8. kǎw tôht ขอโทษ

Meaning – sorry / excuse me

Context – used in the same way as in English – saying sorry or in the verb form, it means to apologise.

Example:

Kǎw tôht <u>ná</u> <u>ká</u>, <u>hâwng</u>-náam yòo taang <u>nǎi</u> <u>ká</u>?

ขอโทษนะคะ ห้องน้ำอยู่ทางไหนคะ

Excuse me, which way is the toilet?

Tips / in my experience / insight: *you cannot use 'kǎw tôht' to sympathise or feel sorrow as 'sorry' can in English.*

9. pŏm / chún / káo ผม / ฉัน / เขา

Meaning – I (male / female) / he / she

Context – these are the most basic personal pronouns; note that *'I'* is a different word for men and women but *'he / she'* is the same word.

Example:
Pŏm mâi kâo jai krúp.

ผมไม่เข้าใจครับ

I don't understand.

Note that the 'kâo' above is NOT the same word as the word for *'he / she'* in the title. This is very important and the only difference in the two words, from a foreigner's perspective, is the difference in tone, which may be barely audible to a beginner's ear. From a Thai person's perspective, there is absolutely no connection or similarity between the two words and they are spelt with different 'k' consonants in Thai. So, as frustrating as it may be, try not to focus too much on the similarity in the transliterated spelling and DO ensure you get the tone correct for each word – they sound nothing like each other to Thais and there is no similarity whatsoever.

Person A: <u>Káo</u> <u>bpen</u> <u>krai</u> <u>ká</u>? Person B: <u>Bpen</u> pôo <u>jàt</u>-gaan <u>krúp</u>.

คนแรก: เขาเป็นใครคะ คนที่สอง: เป็นผู้จัดการครับ

Person A: Who is that? Person B: That is the manager.

Although 'káo' is used for both *'he'* and *'she'*, in many cases it is obvious whether the person being spoken of is male or female and where it is not, Thai people simply use other means such as using the person's name or even not bothering to clarify if it is not important to the point of the sentence.

Tips / in my experience / insight: *here is some good news – personal pronouns are used quite sparingly in Thai and verbs do not have to agree ('I go, he goes' etc.). Look back to entries 6 and 7 for personal pronoun omissions.*

The omission of personal pronouns where it is obvious who the subject is, is a central aspect of Thai speech. In many conversations, you would be hard-pressed to hear 'pŏm' or other pronouns at all, which can make it tricky to know who is talking about who.

Also notice that I have not even bothered with the word for 'you' (which is '_koon_', which btw is also the word for 'Mr.' or 'Mrs.'). This is because it is even rarer to hear this being used because it is almost always superfluous anyway and also because Thais have a range of other alternative personal pronouns they use in everyday speech.

Note however that, in spite of all the above, using these personal pronouns is not wrong and they are not always omitted so if you find yourself saying '_chún_' more often than you hear it back from Thai people, don't stress – you are speaking correctly. In fact, in general, the more verbose a sentence, the more polite it sounds and the more words omitted, the more abrupt it sounds. Thais omit personal pronouns often because of familiarity and informality; you won't be familiar with anybody so not a good idea to be too informal.

10. chôhk dee โชคดี

Meaning – Good luck

Context – Literally, *'good luck'* but often as a casual and warmer alternative to *'goodbye'* and as a generic *"wishing you well"* sentiment. You may well get this from a taxi driver dropping you off at the airport, for example.

Example:
(Taxi driver) Person A: Sèe <u>sìp</u> hâa bàht <u>krúp</u>.
Person B: Kàwb <u>koon</u> krúp. Chôhk dee <u>krúp</u>.

คนแรก: สี่สิบห้าบาทครับ คนที่สอง: ขอบคุณครับ โชคดี

ครับ

(Taxi driver) Person A: 45 baht please. Person B: Thanks. Good luck / All the best.

Tips / in my experience / insight: *and to finish off this chapter let's return to the simplest word – hello. Rather than saying 'sa-wàt dee krúp' to every single person you come across in Thailand, try to vary it a bit. Remember I said before that Thais do not only say "hello" and pretty much never say "good morning" etc.*

So, for example, you could say 'sa-wàt dee krúp' to the maid in your hotel and 'sa-baai dee mái krúp' to the food stall owner you met the day before (because you do not need to start with 'hello' and can jump to 'how are you?' as an opening greeting). Or, 'bpai năi krúp' – 'where are you going' cheekily to the masseuse passing you on the street and who called out 'bpai năi ká' to you yesterday as you walked past. See how it works? Fit in better with just a bit of variation in your words.

2. OTHER COMMON FIRST WORDS

Words covered in this chapter		
cheu	ชื่อ	name
maak	มาก	a lot / very
kon	คน	person / people
paa-saa	ภาษา	language
rot	รถ	car / vehicle
aa-yoo	อายุ	age
jaak	จาก	from
kawng	ของ	word indicating possession

NB: Transliteration above written without tone or other pronunciation marks.

11. chêu ชื่อ

Meaning – name

Context – a rather tricky word to pronounce properly due to the falling tone that does not come naturally to a Western tongue but in terms of meaning and usage, just as in English.

Example:

Chún chêu E-mée kà. Koon chêu a-rai ká?

ฉันชื่อเอมี่ค่ะ คุณชื่ออะไรคะ

My name is Amy. What is your name?

You will be surprised at how this is almost always not the first or second thing in conversations, unlike in the West.

Tips / in my experience / insight: *although the '<u>koon</u>' can be omitted – and often is omitted by Thai people – it is better to err on the side of formality and politeness in your initial attempts at conversation.*

Having said that, if you were to omit the '<u>koon</u>', that would be fine too, especially if the person is of similar or lower age or (in your estimation) of similar social status. So, for example, it would be a little abrupt to say "Chêu <u>a-rai</u> <u>krúp</u>?" to your girlfriend's father or a civil servant but not to a girl in a bar. Ok?

Note also, as you may know already, that Thai names are generally quite long and most Thai people will have a shorter version of their first name or a nickname ('chêu <u>lên</u>' – literally, 'play-name') that they use in everyday situations. You may and probably will get told a

Thai person's nickname in most cases because it will be easier to pronounce in most cases.

Some Thai people may choose to tell you their actual name simply because that is their name after all and / or because the social situation you are in dictates a bit more formality. Whether or not you choose to follow up and enquire if the person has a nickname is up to your judgement at the time. If you do, you can ask *"mee ch~~êu~~ lên mái ká / krúp?"*

Apart from anyone who has become your Thai friend, you should address them with the '*Koon*' prefix, even if it is their nickname.

Finally, to return to the example, note that, just as in English, an alternative way to introduce yourself is 'I'm Amy', which is even easier in Thai – '*chún Amy kà*' (literally, 'I Amy') or '*pŏm Greg krúp*' (literally, 'I Greg').

12. mâak มาก

Meaning – very

Context – this is obviously a very useful word at beginner level as it can be used to be expressive and if pronounced properly, will impress because it is falling tone hence quite different to mid-tone English.

Example:

A̲-ròi mâak.

อร่อยมาก

Delicious!

Add '<u>krúp</u> / <u>ká</u>' when responding to a question or when specifically directing this comment to someone e.g. the host / cook but if making rhetorical statements, leaving out this particle is ok.

Person A: Hĭuw <u>mái</u> <u>ká</u>? Person B: Hĭuw mâak <u>krúp</u>.

คนแรก: หิวไหมคะ คนที่สอง: หิวมากครับ

Person A: Are you hungry? Person B: Starving! Literally, (I am) very hungry!

<u>Gèng</u> mâak.

เก่งมาก

(You are) very clever / good! (at whatever you action you were doing).

You may hear this short phrase in response if you have spoken Thai well. If you don't want to be humble, as is expected in Thailand, in response, you could say "<u>mâi</u> mee <u>a</u>-<u>rai</u> <u>krúp</u>' – *'it was nothing'* – with a look of arrogance or smugness on your face.

Person A: Jèp mâak mái ká? Person B: Mái (jèp) mâak kà. Mâi bpen rai kà.

คนแรก: เจ็บมากไหมคะ คนที่สอง: ไม่ (เจ็บ) มากค่ะ ไม่เป็นไรค่ะ

Person A: Does it hurt a lot? Person B: No, not really, it's nothing.

Notice the literal translation of the question to see how simple it is in Thai – *"Hurt a lot?"* ("mái ká?") are particles with no inherent meaning.

> **Tips / in my experience / insight:** *note that 'mâak' is generally an intensifier for adjectives and you should not confuse it with 'yéuh', which means 'a lot / many' and is more used with verbs and nouns e.g. 'kon yéuh' means 'lots of people'. Generally, 'mâak' is used for non-countable concepts / adjectives whereas 'yéuh' is for more tangible things.*

13. <u>kon</u> คน

Meaning – person / people

Context – clearly a very useful word; learning just a few usages of this word will expand vocabulary rapidly. One simple example is '<u>kon</u> diao', which means *'alone'* or *'by oneself'*.

Example:

<u>Bp</u>en <u>kon</u> <u>bp</u>rà-têt <u>a</u>-<u>rai</u> <u>ká</u>?

เป็นคนประเทศอะไรคะ

What country are you from? What nationality are you?

'<u>Bp</u>rà-têt' means *'country'*. Notice there is no need to say *'you'*, as is common in Thai because it is obvious from the context.

14. paa-săa ภาษา

Meaning – language

Context – a good word to practise pronunciation – the 'săa' is in the rising tone – see if you can hear how it is different to the 'paa' when said by Thais.

Example:
Person A: Pôod paa-săa <u>tai</u> dâai <u>mái</u> <u>krúp</u>?
Person B: <u>Mâi</u> <u>kôi</u> dâai <u>krúp</u>.

คนแรก: พูดภาษาไทยได้ไหมครับ คนที่สอง: ไม่ค่อยได้
ครับ

Person A: Can you speak Thai? Person B: Not really, I'm afraid.

15. <u>rót</u> รถ

Meaning – car / vehicle

Context – '<u>rót</u>' is both a generic word for most types of road and rail vehicle and for *'car'*; the full word for *'car'* is '<u>rót</u>-<u>yon</u>', often shortened to just '<u>rót</u>'. A bus is '<u>rót</u> mae'. (Meanwhile the generic word for a water based vessel is 'reua' i.e. *'boat'*, *'ship'*, *'ferry'*.)

Example:
Person A: <u>Nâng</u> / <u>bpai</u> <u>rót</u>-<u>fai</u>-fáa <u>mái</u>?
Person B: Dee <u>krúp</u> / <u>bpai</u> <u>krúp</u>.

คนแรก: นั่ง / ไปรถไฟฟ้าไหม คนที่สอง: ดีครับ / ไปครับ

Person A: Want to go by skytrain? Person B: Sounds good / yeah, sure.

Notice about the previous sentence:

- You can use '<u>nâng</u>', the verb *'to sit'*, to refer to using the skytrain.
- The Thai version of the sentence is quite a bit simpler than the English; literally, the Thai is *'sit / go skytrain?'* You will have noticed this in many of the sentences so far and is clearly a good thing if you are a beginner learning Thai.
- Finally, notice the response is either to just repeat the verb in the question or just say *"good"*.

Tips / in my experience / insight: *many '<u>rót</u>' conversations require more Thai than at this beginner level so, for this book, the most useful word to learn is '<u>rót dtìd</u>' – 'heavy traffic / traffic jam.' You are pretty much guaranteed to hear it in Bangkok if you travel by road.*

16. aa-yóo อายุ

Meaning – age

Context – unlike in the West, a person's age is a source of some interest in introductory conversations in Thailand. This is a cultural thing and also a factor of practicality in terms of being one (the main) way Thai people decide who has seniority and therefore who is 'pêe' (a prefix indicating being older or having seniority) and who is 'náwng' (the opposite i.e. for someone younger) in a social situation. I will not spend more space here on the prefixes and forms of address between Thai people; readers can ask locals to explain. Usually, they are not used with foreigners anyway.

Having said the above, in general, Thai people do not explicitly ask each other's age (but it is often indirectly referenced and where in doubt, the person who assumes he / she is younger refers to the other as 'pêe' until it is clearer later on who is older) whereas with foreigners it is very often one of the first things they ask. This is usually simply innocent curiosity and one of the cultural norms of polite small talk in initial, non-formal engagements with foreigners.

Example:

Person A: (<u>Koon</u>) aa-<u>yóo</u> <u>tâo</u> <u>rai</u> <u>ká</u>?　Person B: (<u>Pŏm</u>) aa-<u>yóo</u> yêe-<u>sìp</u> <u>jèd</u> bpee <u>krúp</u>.

คนแรก: (คุณ) อายุเท่าไหรคะ คนที่สอง: (ผม) อายุยี่สิบ เจ็ดปีครับ

Person A: How old are you?　Person B: I'm 27 (years old).

17. jàak จาก

Meaning – from

Context – exactly as in English.

Example:

C<u>hún</u> maa jàak Yî-<u>bpòon</u> k<u>à</u>.

ฉันมาจากญี่ปุ่นค่ะ

I am / come from Japan.

Maa jàak <u>jai</u> <u>krúp</u>.

มาจากใจครับ

From the heart.

Say with OTT sincerity to get a laugh.

18. kăwng ของ

Meaning – word indicating possession

Context – in Thai, to indicate something belongs to someone, this word is placed in front of the subject. Often, for brevity and convenience, as seen in many cases already, the word is omitted if it does not affect the meaning.

Example:

(Bpen) toh-ra-sàp (kăwng) krai ká?

(เป็น) โทรศัพท์ (ของ) ใครคะ

Whose phone is this?

As you can see, 'kăwng' can be omitted.

PUTTING IT ALL TOGETHER: SUMMARY OF CHAPTER 1 + 2

This breakout chapter is intended to bring together some of the words of the first two chapters in a representation of a real conversation. Note however that no representation can ever be exactly like a real conversation unless it is a transcript of an actual conversation so you should not be surprised if responses to your attempts do not match what is written here; indeed, this helps to learn more.

The second part of this chapter is to suggest some areas where you can learn more word combinations from the words already given in the first two chapters. As mentioned before, I do not believe in tests in a beginner book / phrasebook – I find them kind of annoying and the best way to test yourself is to go out and speak to Thai people and see their reaction – so these are just pointers for those so inclined or inspired.

Scenario: Chatting with a taxi driver

Driver: <u>Bpai</u> <u>năi</u> <u>krúp</u>?

คนขับรถ: ไปไหนครับ

Driver: Where do you want to go?

You: <u>Bpai</u> <u>sa</u>-năam <u>bin</u> <u>krúp</u>.

คุณ: ไปสนามบินครับ

You: To the airport (whichever one).

(Note that the correct way to pronounce Suvarnabhumi is '<u>Sòo</u>-<u>wan</u>-<u>ná</u>-poom').

You: <u>Rót</u> <u>dtìd</u> <u>mái</u> <u>krúp</u>?

คุณ: รถติดไหมครับ

You: Is there going to be traffic?

Driver: <u>Dtìd</u> <u>krúp</u>. <u>Dtìd</u> <u>tóok</u> <u>wan</u>…

คนขับรถ: ติดครับ ติดทุกวัน…

Driver: Yes, the traffic is bad every day…

Driver: ...Kêun taang dùan mái krúp?

คนขับรถ: ...ขึ้นทางด่วนไหมครับ

Driver: ...Do you want to take the tollway?

You: Dâai krúp.

คุณ: ได้ครับ

You: Yes (literally, "can").

Driver: Maa tîao meuang tai rěuh?

คนขับรถ: มาเที่ยวเมืองไทยเหรอ

Driver: Did you come to Thailand for a holiday?

You: Krúp. Maa tîao săwng săam aa-tíd láeo.

คุณ: ครับ มาเที่ยวสองสามอาทิตย์แล้ว

You: Yep, for about two or three weeks now.

Driver: Láeo <u>bin</u> <u>bpai</u> <u>năi</u> dtàw?

คนขับรถ: แล้วบินไปไหนต่อ

Driver: And where are you flying out to next?

You: <u>Bpai</u> <u>Ang-grìt</u> <u>krúp</u>.

คุณ: ไปอังกฤษครับ

You: To the UK.

Driver: Aaw, <u>bpen</u> <u>kon</u> <u>Ang-grìt</u> rĕuh?

คนขับรถ: อ๋อ เป็นคนอังกฤษเหรอ

Driver: Oh, you're British?

You: <u>Krúp</u>, maa jàak <u>Lawn-dawn</u> <u>krúp</u>.

คุณ: ครับ มาจากลอนดอนครับ

You: Yes, I'm from London.

Notice the Thai does not have the personal pronoun, *'I'* in casual speech.

Driver: <u>Tam</u>-<u>mai</u> pôod <u>tai</u> <u>gèng</u> <u>jung</u>?

คนขับรถ: ทำไมพูดไทยเก่งจัง

Driver: How come you can speak Thai so well?

Thais are impressed with an attempt at a few words in Thai from foreigners and will often generously call you '<u>gèng</u>' (*'smart / clever'*).

You: <u>Mâi</u> gèng ràwk. Kàwp <u>koon</u> <u>krúp.</u>

คุณ: ไม่เก่งหรอก ขอบคุณครับ

You: No, I'm not that good but thank you.

Driver: <u>Gèng</u>, gèng. Maa tîao <u>bòi</u> <u>châi</u> <u>mái</u> <u>krúp</u>?

คนขับรถ: เก่ง เก่ง มาเที่ยวบ่อยใช่ไหมครับ

Driver: No, your Thai is good! You must have come here for holiday many times, right?

You: Bòi krúp. Pǒm châwp tîao meuang tai mâak.

คุณ: บ่อยครับ ผมชอบเที่ยวเมืองไทยมาก

You: Yeah, I love travelling around Thailand.

Driver: Láeo jà glàp maa tîao èeg mêua-rai krúp?

คนขับรถ: แล้วจะกลับมาเที่ยวอีกเมื่อไหร่ครับ

Driver: So when are you coming back?

You: Yang mâi róo krúp.

คุณ: ยังไม่รู้ครับ

You: Not sure yet.

Driver: Gâw glàp maa reo reo láeo gun ná krúp. Chôhk dee krúp.

คนขับรถ: ก็กลับมาเร็ว ๆ แล้วกันนะครับ โชคดีครับ

Driver: Come back as soon as you can then. All the best.

Tips / in my experience / insight: *possibly the best tip I can give you in terms of learning Thai is to speak to taxi drivers. You have a captive audience for starters and you also may not know too many other Thai people anyway if you are on holiday. No matter how little Thai you can speak, taxi drivers are probably the best people to ask your questions to and practise with (unless, of course, you get a driver in a bad mood!).*

Some thoughts on further learning

As I mentioned earlier, I do not like tests and exercises, especially in beginner level books, for the obvious reason that, in most cases, you, the reader, do not want to become a student of Thai. You simply want to learn some simple words and phrases and learn enough of basic grammar to be able to say a sentence in Thai now and then to impress your Thai friends or hosts which can then often lead onto a conversation (in English) about a particular Thai word and how to pronounce it and how it is used; this is how most beginners learn).

But of course, there are those of you who will start reading this book and really get into it and find it relatively easy to pick up the basic structures of Thai (because they are rea- sonably simple in reality). To address this, beyond the pointers in this section, I recommend you purchase **Essential Thai** by **James Higbie**. It is by far and away the best basic Thai book out there.

For now, I can give you a little insight into how I learnt Thai. No book will ever give you every single combination of words pre- sented in just the order that you need them in your particular situation so while, yes, you do need to memorise words you have read, you also need to work out, for yourself, how to combine words and figure out patterns in order to make real progress towards forming sentences. Don't know what I mean? Here are some ideas to get you started:

- Do you know the word for *"his"* or *"her"* in Thai? Clue: you should be able to work it out using words 18 and 9. Got it?

- How would you say *"I'm not hungry"* in Thai? Clue: I have given you the Thai for *"I am hungry"* and before that, I have given you the word for *"not"* to make it a negative statement.

- Now that you know the word for *"not"*, you can add this in front of any adjective you hear or learn from your conversations in Thailand and instantly learn the opposite of that adjective e.g. *"not cold"*, *"not good"*, *"not hot"* etc.

- Similarly, you should now be able to intensify just about any adjective you learn / hear. So you should be able to say *"very fast"*, *"very hot"*, *"very good"* etc, greatly expanding your vocabulary.

- The word for *"to joke"* in Thai is "pôod lên". Can you see why? You should be able to because I have used both of these words separately previously.

- Keep going in this vein and you will see that even the few Thai words I have given you so far in the first two chapters are enough to allow you to deduce many more simple words and expressions. Try it.

Tips / in my experience / insight: *probably unlike any other book in the market, I would actually encourage you to speak English in Thailand! This is for several reasons:*

1) you will get more out of Thailand by engaging with local people and not letting the language barrier get in the way,

2) approaching in your own language will give you more confidence (from where you can throw in a few attempts at Thai once you have got past hello etc. and

3) Thai people generally do want to practise their English. Some of the best conversations you will have on your trip to Thailand will be where you mix English and Thai and have fun learning each other's language. Remember: speak English in a neutral accent, minimize metaphors, idioms, esoteric references etc.

3. ALL THE VERBS YOU NEED

Words covered in this chapter		
bpai	ไป	to go
chawp	ชอบ	to like
maa	มา	to come
yoo	อยู่	to be located at / to live
bpen	เป็น	to be
seu	ซื้อ	to buy
lot	ลด	to discount / reduce
tiao	เที่ยว	to go out
doo	ดู	to look / watch
yaak / ao	อยาก / เอา	to want / to want
tam	ทำ	to do / make
gin	กิน	to eat / to consume
mee	มี	to have
roo / roo jak	รู้ / รู้จัก	to know
kao jai	เข้าใจ	to understand
pood	พูด	to speak / say

NB: Transliteration above written without tone or other pronunciation marks.

19. <u>bpai</u> ไป

Meaning – to go

Context – the same as in English but as may have been noticed already, in Thai the *"to"* after *"go"* is often omitted for brevity and convenience as it does not add anything to the meaning. This is a key feature of Thai speech and indeed, Thai culture and mentality that is key for foreigners to understand; in short, 'keep it simple'. Everyday speech, especially in informal situations amongst people who know each other already, often omits superfluous words. Compared to English, this makes learning Thai easier as the grammar is simpler – less fussy prepositions and so on.

Example:

Person A: <u>Bpai</u> <u>gin</u> kâao <u>gun</u> <u>mái</u>? Person B: <u>Bpai</u>…hĭuw. <u>Bpai</u> <u>năi</u> dee? Person A: <u>Bpai</u> <u>Cen</u>-tûn <u>gun</u> <u>mái</u>?

คนแรก: ไปกินข้าวกันไหม   คนที่สอง: ไป…หิว ไปไหนดี

คนแรก: ไป เซ็นทรัลกันไหม

Person A: Shall we go get something to eat? Person B: Yeah, I'm hungry. Where shall we go? Person A: What about Central (Mall)?

Yàak <u>bpai</u> tîao <u>Poo</u>-gèt <u>mái</u>?

อยากไปเที่ยวภูเก็ตไหม

Want to go on a trip to Phuket?

Notice I have not bothered adding '<u>jà</u>' in front of '<u>bpai</u>' to indicate future tense because it is obviously a future tense question.

20. châwp ชอบ

Meaning – to like

Context – the key with this and generally with falling tone words is to put the effort in to get the tone right. It can be a bit embarrassing to a Westerner as it sounds whiny but getting over this and not pronouncing in an 'English way' is critical to getting credibility.

Example:

Def châwp gin aa-hăan tai mái ká?

เดฟชอบกินอาหารไทยไหมคะ

Do you like Thai food Dave?

21. maa มา

Meaning – to come

Context – clearly a straightforward word but it is also used to indicate the present perfect tense as shown in the first example.

Example:

Person A: Bpai tîao năi maa? Person B: Bpai Chiang-Mài maa kà.

คนแรก: ไปเที่ยวไหนมา คนที่สอง: ไปเชียงใหม่มาค่ะ

Person A: Where have you been (travelling)? Person B: Chiang-Mai.

Note that 'tîao' in the question doesn't necessarily mean the questioner knows that you have been out travelling or out last night or whatever, it is just assumed as a way of being affectionate or warm. Obviously, you could just as commonly be asked without the 'tîao' i.e. "bpai năi maa?"

Also notice the way you say where you have come back from – 'bpai maa' – literally, *'go come (back from)'*. Just put the name of the place between the two and you can talk about where you have returned from.

You will hear people asking other people "bpai năi maa?" as a common greeting. It does not necessarily mean they need to know all the finer details of your day so far, it is just a friendly thing Thais say. If you don't want to specify, you can just say "mâi dâi bpai năi kà" – *"nowhere"*.

Maa nâng doo rôop bpai tîao gun.

มานั่งดูรูปไปเที่ยวกัน

Come and sit down and take a look at our photos from the trip.

78

Tips / in my experience / insight: *the previous sentence shows you the beauty of Thai for foreigners trying to learn the language. A lot of the grammar can be amazingly simple and can be reduced to just the words that are necessary. So with Thai you can say the bare minimum and have a chance of being understood. Great for beginners!*

When in doubt, give it a go! You never know, you may get near enough to your meaning if you know the key adjective or verb. Yes, the pronunciation is tricky but don't be put off. Give it a go and you will be rewarded with warm appreciation. And where you do get confusion or misunderstanding, don't worry. Just relax and listen out for the right way to say what you tried to say for the next time. Of course, you can also persevere and ask (in English) what you said wrong but often this leads to further confusion! All part of the fun.

22. yòo อยู่

Meaning – to be located at / to live

Context – when a question or statement refers to your location, you do not use the verb to be (is, am, are) but use this verb (see below). 'yòo' is also used to indicate the present continuous tense by adding it behind the verb.

Example:

Person A: <u>Káo</u> yòo têe-<u>nai</u>? Person B: Yòo bâan (<u>káo</u>).

คนแรก: เขาอยู่ที่ไหน คนที่สอง: อยู่บ้าน(เขา)

Person A: Where is he / she? Person B: At (his / her) home.

Gin a-rai yòo ká?

กินอะไรอยู่คะ

What are you eating?

Kùp rót yòo.

ขับรถอยู่

I'm driving.

Person A: Kăw tôht ná krúp, wan née, Meaw yòo mái krúp? Person B: Mâi yòo kà. Wan Jan Meaw mâi maa tam ngaan.

คนแรก: ขอโทษนะครับ วันนี้แมวอยู่ไหมครับ คนที่สอง:
ไม่อยู่ค่ะ วันจันทร์แมวไม่มาทำงาน

Person A: Excuse me, is Meaw in today? Person B: No she isn't, Meaw doesn't work Mondays.

If you want to enquire after a girl in a bar.

23. <u>bpen</u> เป็น

Meaning – to be

Context – another word that is often omitted where it adds no value to the sentence e.g. the Thai for *"I am hungry"* (as seen in word 12) is just *"I hungry"*.

Example:

<u>Bpen</u> (<u>yang</u>) <u>ngai</u>?

เป็น (ยัง) ไง

How's things?

A more informal way of saying *"how are you?"* (word 7); you can also omit the '<u>yang</u>' where you know the other person well and can speak casually.

24. séu ซื้อ

Meaning – to buy

Context – Thailand is known for its shopping so this word is quite useful.

Example:

Séu maa tâo rai?

ซื้อมาเท่าไหร่

How much did you buy it for / was it?

Bpai séu kăwng gun.

ไปซื้อของกัน

Let's go shopping.

25. <u>lót</u> ลด

Meaning – to discount / reduce

Context – clearly a useful word for Thailand where shopping is so attractive a pastime, especially in a hot and humid country where being indoors in a shopping mall makes more sense albeit, bargaining is more relevant for markets and streetside vendors.

It is worth bearing in mind that when trying to bargain with a street vendor, the amount of the discount is often quite small in Western terms and any negotiation should lead to BOTH parties being happy so it is not wise to demand discounts or continue to haggle aggressively when the seller has confirmed that he will not go any lower. It makes little difference in pounds or dollars and it is really not worth the ill feeling. If you really think you are being ripped off, walk away. Better for both sides. If you do barter, do it with good humour and be friendly.

Example:

(Chûai) <u>lót</u> <u>hâi</u> <u>nòi</u> <u>ná</u> <u>krúp</u> / <u>Lót</u> (raa-kaa) dâai <u>mái</u> <u>krúp</u>? / <u>Lót</u> dâai <u>tâo</u> <u>rai</u> <u>krúp</u>?

(ช่วย) ลดให้หน่อยนะครับ / ลด (ราคา) ได้ไหมครับ / ลด ได้เท่าไหร่ครับ

Could you pls reduce it a little / Can you give me a discount? / What can you do (on the price)?

The above can often be followed up by '(insert desired price) dâai <u>mái</u> <u>ká</u>?' Check out the chapter on numbers to be able to say prices in Thai. It's easy!

26. tîao เที่ยว

Meaning – to go out

Context – there is no exact equivalent to this word in English as it covers all kinds of going out such as going out to a shopping mall or for 'nightlife' or to another province or country as a tourist or pretty much any type of outing.

Example:

Tîao tóok wan leuy!

เที่ยวทุกวันเลย

I am out every single day!

Declare this and get a few laughs.

27. doo ดู

Meaning – to look / watch

Context – a simple and useful word.

Example:
Bpai doo năng gun mái krúp?

ไปดูหนังกันไหมครับ

Would you like to go watch a film?

Doo gàwn krúp.

ดูก่อนครับ

Let's (wait and) see. (Literally, 'look before').

Use this to politely decline going in / buying.

28. yàak / <u>ao</u> อยาก / เอา

Meaning – to want to / to want

Context – there are two main words for the verb to want. The difference between them is what things are being wanted: yàak is used with verbs and so is 'to want to' while <u>ao</u> is used with nouns and adjectives.

Example:

Yàak mee faen <u>jung</u>!

อยากมีแฟนจัง

I really want a girlfriend / boyfriend! Another phrase that is a bit comical and can be said with mock excessive angst to make locals laugh.

Person A: <u>Ao</u> <u>a-rai</u> <u>mái</u> <u>ká</u>? Person B: <u>Ao</u> dtua née <u>kà</u>. Person A: <u>Ao</u> gèe dtua <u>ká</u>? Person B: <u>Ao</u> săwng dtua <u>kà</u>. S<s>éu</s> <u>hâi</u> p<s>êu</s>an dûai.

คนแรก: เอาอะไรไหมคะ คนที่สอง: เอาตัวนี้ค่ะ คนแรก: เอากี่ตัวคะ คนที่สอง: เอาสองตัวค่ะ ซื้อให้เพื่อนด้วย

Person A: What would you like? Person B: Can I have this one please. Person A: How many do you want? Person B: Can I have two please. I want to get one for my friend too.

In the above example, '<u>ao</u>' means *'want'* in the sense of *"I'll take this one"*. Thais will tell you '<u>ao</u>' means *'take'* but in English, it is closer to *'I want'* or *'I would like'* etc.

(Ordering food) <u>Ao</u> kâao <u>kài</u> jiao <u>kà</u>.

เอาข้าวไข่เจียวค่ะ

Can I have / I would like omelette on rice.

89

29. tam ทำ

Meaning – to do / make

Context – ubiquitous in Thai; learn it.

Example:
Lêuhk ngaan réu yang ká?

เลิกงานหรือยังคะ

Have you finished work yet?

Tam a-rai yòo krúp?

ทำอะไรอยู่ครับ

What are you doing?

30. <u>gin</u> กิน

Meaning – to eat / to consume

Context – used not just for eating and often drinking, more often than 'd~~eu~~m'.

Example:

<u>Gin</u> kâao (<u>ré~~u~~</u>) <u>yang</u>?

กินข้าว (หรือ) ยัง

Have you eaten yet? (Serves as a proxy for a generic and warmer greeting).

Tips / in my experience / insight: *you are likely to hear the more polite and formal alternative for 'eat' – 'taan'.*

31. mee มี

Meaning – to have

Context – used more widely in Thai.

Example:

Mee 'cawn-<u>têek</u> <u>len</u>' <u>mái</u> <u>ká</u>?

มีคอนแทคเลนส์ไหมคะ

Do you have contact lenses?

While there are many ways to enquire whether a store or street vendor sells a particular product, this is probably the simplest. (One alternative is "Hǎa..." – *"I'm looking for..."*.) Note, as mentioned before, the seller will respond "mee" to the example question if he / she does sell it, not "<u>châi</u>".

<u>Mâi</u> mee <u>a-rai</u>.

ไม่มีอะไร

It's nothing / It's not important.

<u>Mâi</u> mee <u>krai</u> yòo (bâan).

ไม่มีใครอยู่ (บ้าน)

There is no-one here / no-one's home (with the word for house in the brackets included).

Note that the main difference between the Thai and the English above is that in Thai you use the verb *'to have'* whereas in English you use the verb *'to be'*. So, in Thai the literal translation is *"this place has nobody"* or, in the Thai word order *"not have someone located"*. In Thai, the verb *'to be'* is used when talking about people's properties and characteristics etc, not if they are present in a location.

Tips / in my experience / insight: *at this point let me go on a slight diversion and explain confirm a few basic points on the verb to have, especially in relation to ordering at a restaurant.*

As we have seen already, to order you need to use 'ao' followed by what you want to order.

For requests (for you to get something or for permission to do something), you need to use the word 'kǎw' – 'to beg', which we have met already in the word for 'sorry' – 'kǎw tôht', which literally means "beg to be punished / blamed". Sometimes you will hear people using 'kǎw' in restaurants, as opposed to 'ao' but this is often in situations where you are requesting ice for your water (or beer!), the WIFI password and suchlike, not ordering things on a menu.

*Finally, you should have figured out by now that you cannot literally translate "Can I have" from English because 'kǎw' already incorporates the "have" so you would **not** say "kǎw mee".*

Although the general advice is not to attempt to translate an English sentence word for word into Thai in the English sentence order as it will almost certainly be incorrect or misunderstood, as mentioned previously, what you can do often is to strip out the prepositions and articles and so on and just speak in the simplest terms and you may well be saying Thai correctly. For example, "I go", "I hungry", "why go?" and so on. So, as a beginner, if you want to attempt to speak a short sentence or two, you have a good chance of getting it right by just looking up the noun, adjective and / or verb in a dictionary and giving it a go.

32. róo / róo-jàk รู้ / รู้จัก

Meaning – to know

Context – these two similar words in Thai have the same meaning but in different contexts: 'róo' refers to knowing a particular point or information or a state of affairs while 'róo-jàk' refers to knowing a person or place or thing.

Example:

Jawn róo-jàk Loso mái krúp?

จอห์นรู้จักโลโซไหมครับ

Do you know (the band) Loso, John?

Remember, repeat the verb to say *'yes'*.

<u>Mâi</u> mee <u>krai</u> róo.

ไม่มีใครรู้

Nobody knows.

Notice again how *'nobody'* in Thai is, in literal terms *"there is nobody"*.

Róo mâak!

รู้มาก

Smarty pants! / Nosy Parker! or other similar retorts. Literally, 'know a lot (too much)!'.

(To taxi driver) Róo-<u>jàk</u> Man U <u>mái</u> <u>krúp</u>?

รู้จักแมนยูไหมครับ

Do you know Man U?

Well worth trying this question as Thais love their football, especially Premiership footy.

33. <u>kâo jai</u> เข้าใจ

Meaning – to understand

Context – obviously a very commonly used word in conversations between Thai locals and foreigners who are beginners in speaking Thai. Note that the Thai is a literal translation of how a person understands: *"enter mind"*. Btw, '<u>jai</u>' means both *'heart'* and *'mind'*.

Example:

Kăw tôht <u>pŏm</u> <u>mâi</u> <u>kâo</u> <u>jai</u> <u>krúp</u>.

ขอโทษ ผมไม่เข้าใจครับ

Sorry, I don't understand.

34. pôod พูด

Meaning – to speak / say

Context – and finally, a verb that has been mentioned several times already, the verb to speak or to say.

Example:
Kăw tôht <u>ná kà</u>, <u>koon</u> pôod paa-săa <u>Ang-grìd</u> dâai <u>mái ká</u>?

ขอโทษนะ คุณพูดภาษาอังกฤษได้ไหมคะ

Excuse me, do you speak English?

An even more polite way to approach somebody with this question is by using '<u>mâi</u> sâap wâa' before '<u>koon</u>'. It means *'I don't know whether… / I was wondering whether…'*

4. EXPRESSING YOURSELF / ADJECTIVES

	Words covered in this chapter	
paeng	แพง	expensive
sa-baai	สบาย	comfortable / pleasant
sa-nook	สนุก	fun / enjoyable
rawn	ร้อน	hot
naao / yen	หนาว / เย็น	cold
jai dee	ใจดี	kind / nice
jai yen	ใจเย็น	calm
dee jai	ดีใจ	very happy / delighted
yai	ใหญ่	big
lek	เล็ก	small
reo	เร็ว	fast
chaa	ช้า	slow

NB: Transliteration above written without tone or other pronunciation marks.

35. paeng แพง

Meaning – expensive

Context – obviously a useful word for shopping – try not to just bluntly blurt this word out to vendors!

Example:

Person A: Ooh, châwp dtua née, <u>Koon</u> Saa-ráa <u>kíd</u> <u>yang</u> <u>ngai?</u> Person B: Châwp <u>kà</u> dtàe paeng <u>bpai</u> <u>mái</u> <u>ká?</u>

คนแรก: โห ชอบตัวนี้ คุณซ่ารา คิดยังไง คนที่สอง: ชอบ

ค่ะ แต่แพงไปไหมคะ

Person A: Oh, I like this one. What do you think Sarah? Person B: Yeah, it's nice but a bit pricy don't you think?

36. <u>sa</u>-baai สบาย

Meaning – comfortable / pleasant

Context – this word is about as central to Thai philosophy of life as it gets. Although it literally means *'comfortable'*, its usage in Thai is a wider concept of being easy-going and at peace etc…so is often seen in names of seaside hotels or massage parlours.

Example:

<u>Bpai</u> nûat táao <u>sa</u>-baai <u>sa</u>-baai <u>gun</u>.

ไปนวดเท้าสบาย ๆ กัน

Let's get a foot massage and relax.

The '<u>gun</u>' is a particle to indicate *'together'*.

37. <u>sa</u>-<u>nòok</u> สนุก

Meaning – fun / enjoyable

Context – many guides to Thailand will say this word describes the very essence of Thai people and culture. Whether or not this is true or a bit of an exaggeration of Thai people's easy-going character, it is still a key word to learn in order to interact with locals.

Example:

<u>Bpen</u> <u>ngai</u> <u>Sà</u>-dtèef, tîao <u>sa</u>-<u>nòok</u> <u>mái</u> <u>ká</u>?

เป็นไง สตีฟ เที่ยวสนุกไหมคะ

How's it going Steve? Having fun?

Because you are a foreigner to Thailand, you will often get this kind of greeting i.e. the questioner does not necessarily know your exact recent activities but just assumes you have been out somewhere as you are on holiday.

If you have been out (and perhaps even if you have not but don't want to bother explaining), the simple response is just to repeat the adjective.

Obviously, you cannot ask the same question to a native Thai...unless, of course, you know that he / she has indeed been out or travelling recently.

Yàak doo <u>nǎng</u> <u>sa-nòok</u> <u>sa-nòok</u> bâang.

อยากดูหนังสนุก ๆ บ้าง

I want to catch a movie sometime...something fun.

See? 'yàak' is always followed by a verb.

38. ráwn ร้อน

Meaning – hot

Context – used for temperature, not to describe spicy food.

Example:

<u>Wan</u> née aa-gàat ráwn mâak.

วันนี้อากาศร้อนมาก

The weather is really hot today.

<u>Ao</u> Laa-dté ráwn <u>kà</u>.

เอาลาเต้ร้อนค่ะ

Can I have a hot Latté.

39. năo / <u>yen</u> หนาว / เย็น

Meaning – cold

Context – the two versions of *'cold'* are for whether you are describing feeling cold (năo) or whether you want to express that something is cold (<u>yen</u>). Interestingly, there is a third usage of *'cold'* in English – as in getting a cold – where in Thai, it is – '(<u>bpen</u>) <u>wàt</u>'.

Example:

Năo <u>jung</u>! M~~eu~~ <u>yen</u>.

หนาวจัง มือเย็น

It's freezing! My hands are cold.

40. jai dee ใจดี

Meaning – kind / nice

Context – as should be obvious already, 'jai' plays a big part in Thai philosophy and this word is one of the many, many derivatives of 'jai'; literally it means *"good heart"*.

Example:

Kon Thai jai dee.

คนไทยใจดี

Thai people are nice.

A simple sentence that is absolutely bound to win you friends so use it! Thais love their country dearly so any praise about how 'sa-baai' it is is always welcomed warmly.

41. <u>jai yen</u> ใจเย็น

Meaning – calm

Context – another word that goes to the heart of Thai philosophy and values – being calm and not getting angry too easily (and showing it). As hard as it might be, worth keeping your frustrations with Thailand in check and if you complain, do it gently.

Example:

Person A: <u>Rót</u> <u>dtìd</u> mâak! Person B: <u>Jai</u> <u>yen</u> <u>yen</u>, dĭao <u>jà</u> <u>tĕung</u> láeo.

คนแรก: รถติดมาก คนที่สอง: ใจเย็น ๆ เดี๋ยวจะถึงแล้ว

Person A: The traffic is a nightmare! Person B: Relax, we're nearly there.

42. dee jai ดีใจ

Meaning – very happy / delighted

Context – more often heard in casual conversation than the less expressive word for *'happy'*, which is 'mee kwaam sòok'. Generally, Thai is a more expressive language than the more conservative and reserved English so can be more fun to copy and reproduce because you can be more flamboyant in your speech.

Example:

Dee jai dûai!

ดีใจด้วย!

Congratulations / Delighted for you!

43. yài ใหญ่

Meaning – big

Context – pretty simple one here.

Example:

Mee 'sái' yài mái krúp?

มีไซซ์ใหญ่ไหมครับ

Do you have this in a bigger size?

Bpai tîao tá-le mái? Bpai Hàad Yài gun.

ไปเที่ยวทะเลไหม ไปหาดใหญ่กัน

Shall we go to the seaside? Let's go to Hat Yai.

44. **lék** เล็ก

Meaning – small

Context – quite simple again but do try to get the tone right i.e. make the effort to go upwards with your tone; anecdotally, pronouncing this with a low tone means you are saying *'iron'*!

Example:

Gâeo lék rěu gâeo yài ká?

แก้วเล็กหรือแก้วใหญ่คะ

Small or large (cup)?

This is what Thai people are asked by the café staff when they order coffee.

45. <u>reo</u> เร็ว

Meaning – fast

Context – another word that can be doubled up as shown below.

Example:

Maa <u>těung</u> <u>reo</u> <u>jung</u>.

มาถึงเร็วจัง

You got here quick.

<u>Gin</u> kâao <u>reo</u> <u>reo</u> <u>sì</u>; <u>fon</u> <u>dtòk</u> láeo.

กินข้าวเร็ว ๆ สิ ฝนตกแล้ว

Eat up, it's starting to rain.

46. cháa ช้า

Meaning – slow

Context – get the high tone right otherwise you will be saying *'numb'*!

Example:

Chûai pôod cháa cháa <u>nòi</u> <u>ná</u> <u>krúp</u>.

ช่วยพูดช้า ๆ หน่อยนะครับ

Please speak a bit more slowly.

Tips / in my experience / insight: *although I learnt this phrase, it is of limited use if you are a beginner and you still can't understand a slower version of whatever was said!*

PUTTING IT ALL TOGETHER: SUMMARY OF CHAPTER 3 + 4

This breakout chapter is a summary of Chapters 3 and 4, which were on fundamental verbs and adjectives right across the Thai language. It would not be practical to construct something that would bring most of these into a single conversation that does not duplicate the example sentences too much, unlike the first two chapters, which were on introductory words.

So instead, let's reinforce a few points that will help you to create your own sentences and understand the previous two chapters better. However, I will keep it brief because this book is targeted at beginners and I recognize that not everyone will want to study Thai; for those that do, a basic Thai course is the best next step. In my opinion, the best book in the market, by a long way, is **Essential Thai** by **James Higbie,** so if anybody reading this book is inspired to want to go a little further, I can assure you there is no better book to give an overview of the basics of everyday Thai language.

In the meantime, here are some points that should help:

- We have seen it a couple of times already but to reiterate, adding 'jà' in front of a verb makes the sentence future tense. However Thai everyday speech is all about keeping it simple and unfussy so where it is obvious that the context is future tense, the 'jà' may be omitted.
- Past tense is indicated by the specification of the time when the verb happened, just as in English. But unlike English, the verb does not change (like *'go'* changes to *'went'*) so

it is a lot easier in Thai in that respect.

- We have met the present perfect several times already. It is a bit trickier to pick up this tense but again, at least there are no verb forms to memorise as there are in English. So, *'I have gone'* is '(bpai láeo', which is literally *'go already'* and *'I have been'* is 'kuey bpai láeo', which is literally *'ever go already'*. Note, as I said earlier, you may do better not omitting the *'I'* when new to Thailand.

- The present continuous is achieved by adding 'yòo' after the verb.

- A question that involves a verb should usually be answered by repeating the verb if the answer is *'yes'* and adding 'mâi' in front of the repeated verb to mean *'no'*.

- Similar rules apply to questions with adjectives. Remember, '<u>châi</u>' is more like *'yes, that's true'* rather than just *'yes'* so it is used more when agreeing with something someone has said. Similarly, '<u>mâi</u>' is more like *'not'* than *'no'* so you need to repeat the adjective or verb after it to complete the negative response.

- Adjectives come after the noun they are describing in Thai word order.

- Thai does not have single word / suffix particle comparatives and superlatives but it is still not too difficult. For comparatives, add 'gwàa' after your adjective and for superlatives, add 'têe <u>sóot</u>', or sometimes, just '<u>sóot</u>' for short.

5. FOOD AND RESTAURANT WORDS

Words covered in this chapter		
aa-haan	อาหาร	food
hiuw	หิว	hungry
naam...	น้ำ...	water...
a-roi	อร่อย	delicious
Im	อิ่ม	full (from eating)
pet	เผ็ด	spicy / hot
waan	หวาน	sweet
kuat	ขวด	bottle
jaan	จาน	plate / dish
gai...	ไก่	chicken...
som dtam	ส้มตำ	papaya salad
kaao mun gai	ข้าวมันไก่	chicken rice
kai	ไข่	egg
ga-fae	กาแฟ	coffee
ka-nom bpang bping	ขนมปังปิ้ง	toast
guay dtiao	ก๋วยเตี๋ยว	noodle soup
kaao / kaao pad	ข้าว / ข้าวผัด	rice / fried rice

NB: Transliteration above written without tone or other pronunciation marks.

A quick note before we start this chapter. Since many of the words are just straight-forward nouns, do not require any particular explanation and several of them have already been mentioned in previous chapters, I will skip the example sentences for those words.

Second, you will have noticed in this chapter (as well as in previous chapters) that for several of the Thai words, I have listed two or more alternatives and still counted it as one word (of the total 100 words). Not only is this good value for money for you :) as a reader but it gives you similar words in one listing. It would have been easily possible but farcical to fill up half the book with food words listed individually. So, again, in the numbers section later, I have listed 0 to 10 as one 'word', for example.

47. aa-hǎan อาหาร

Meaning – food

Context – we have already met this word and it is mentioned several times later in the book so the only point that is worth re-iterating is that in everyday language you are more likely to hear "gin kâao réu yang?" rather than 'aa-hǎan', which is a bit formal; 'kâao' is used as a synonym for food or a meal.

48. hǐuw หิว

Meaning – hungry

49. náam... น้ำ...

Meaning – water (náam bplào)... / generic prefix for many types of liquid

Context – as well as the drinks below that all begin with the word 'náam', so do *'tears'*, *'dipping sauce'* etc.

Náam <u>sôm</u>	น้ำส้ม	*Orange juice*
<u>Nom</u>	นม	*Milk*
<u>Lâo</u>	เหล้า	*Whisky*
Bia	เบียร์	*Beer*
Wai	ไวน์	*Wine*

Note: Singha Beer in Thai is pronounced 'Bia <u>Sĭng</u>'. The 'ha' is silent and '<u>Sĭng</u>' rising tone.

50. a-ròi อร่อย

Meaning – delicious

51. ìm อิ่ม

Meaning – full (from eating)

Context – an easy word post meal.

Example:

Ìm láeo.

อิ่มแล้ว

I'm full / done.

52. <u>pèt</u> เผ็ด

Meaning – spicy / hot

Context – obviously a word bound to come up in initial meal experiences.

Example:

Jawn <u>gin</u> aa-hăan <u>pèt</u> dâai <u>mái</u> <u>ká</u>?.

จอห์น กินอาหารเผ็ดได้ไหมคะ

Are you ok with spicy food John?

Aa-hăan <u>tai</u> <u>pèt</u> <u>nòi</u> <u>ná</u> <u>ká</u>.

อาหารไทยเผ็ดหน่อยนะคะ

Thai food can be quite spicy, you know.

126

53. **wăan** หวาน

Meaning – sweet

54. **kùat** ขวด

Meaning – bottle

Context – just as in English

Example:
Ao bia săwng kùat krúp.

เอาเบียร์สองขวดครับ

Can I have two bottles of beer please.

55. jaan จาน

Meaning – plate / dish

Context – both a noun and classifier.

Example:

Ao kâao gèe jaan ká?

เอาข้าวกี่จานคะ

How many rice (orders) do you want?

Kăw kâao èeg jaan neung krúp.

ขอข้าวอีกจานหนึ่งครับ

Can I have another plate of rice please.

56. gài... ไก่

Meaning – chicken...

Context – ...and the rest of the main meat and fish words are:

| Néua | เนื้อ | *Beef* |

'Néua' is the generic word for meat and is used as a prefix with the name of the animal following it to be more specific; in everyday usage, 'néua' is used for *'beef'* and people do not bother with saying 'wua' – *'cow'* after.

| Mŏo | หมู | *Pork* |

| Gôong | กุ้ง | *Prawn* |

| Bplaa | ปลา | *Fish* |

57. <u>sôm</u> <u>dtam</u> ส้มตำ

Meaning – green papaya salad

Context – an absolute staple of Thai food from the Northeast of Thailand; a must try!

58. kâao <u>mun</u> <u>gài</u> ข้าวมันไก่

Meaning – chicken rice

Context – this may be the best and simplest dish in Thailand and it is generally not available in the West!

59. kài ไข่

Meaning – egg

60. ga-fae กาแฟ

Meaning – coffee ('ráwn' – *'hot'* or 'yen' – *'cold'* or *'iced'* in this context)

61. kà-nŏm bpang bpîng ขนมปังปิ้ง

Meaning – toast

62. gŭay dtĭao ก๋วยเตี๋ยว

Meaning – noodle soup

Context – what would Thailand be without 'gŭay dtĭao' (like imagining Japan without Ramen!). There is an absolute myriad of varieties that I will not go into here; exploring these is half the fun of Thailand – ask a Thai friend to explain the main types. By default, it is soup-based noodles but you can non-soup, 'dry' versions: 'gŭay dtĭao hâeng'.

63. kâao / kâao <u>pad</u> ข้าว / ข้าวผัด

Meaning – rice / fried rice

Tips / in my experience / insight: *Thai food, usually dinner with several people, is meant to be shared. People do not just order their own thing as they do in the West.*

You may be asked whether you are ok with spicy food and have you ever had this or that before but other than that, the very best thing you can do is to stay out of the ordering process. Just tell your Thai friends that they are the experts and let them order for you and you are happy to try whatever they order.

Nobody will stop you ordering your own thing obviously but it is in your own interest to fit in to the central aspect of Thai social life: eating together and sharing food is key to that.

Obviously, all this does not apply to noodles or one plate dishes for lunch.

6. ASKING BASIC QUESTIONS

Words covered in this chapter		
mai	ไหม	question particle
reu bplao	หรือเปล่า	or not?
tao rai	เท่าไหร่	how much?
tee nai	ที่ไหน	where?
tam-mai	ทำไม	why?
yang ngai	ยังไง	how?
meua rai	เมื่อไหร่	when?
krai	ใคร	who?
gee	กี่	how many?
a-rai	อะไร	what?
...nai	...ไหน	which...?

NB: *Transliteration above written without tone or other pronunciation marks.*

64. <u>mái</u> ไหม

Meaning – question particle

Context – we have seen this word many times already so it should be obvious by now how it works – simply add at the end of a statement to convert it to a question i.e. think of the word for *'hot'* and add '<u>mái</u>' and you have *"are you hot?"*.

Example:

<u>Bpai</u> <u>gin</u> <u>lâo</u> <u>gun</u> <u>mái</u>?!

ไปกินเหล้ากันไหม

Shall we go get drunk?!

Literally, *'go drink whisky together?'*

65. <u>réu</u> bplào หรือเปล่า

Meaning – or not?

Context – although it may seem a bit blunt to ask someone a question ending with "*...or not?*" in English, in Thai, it is not rude and is just a way of being a bit more direct with your question than '<u>mái</u>'. Always add the politeness particle to soften the directness.

Example:

<u>Jing</u> <u>réu</u> bplào <u>krúp</u>?

จริงหรือเปล่าครับ

Is that right? / Is that true? Really?

This is a commonly heard semi-rhetorical expression in Thailand.

A variant is 'jing rĕuh?'. (Note that I have spelt 'rĕuh?' with an 'r' but when spoken, it is usually pronounced with an 'l'.

In certain Asian languages, 'l' and 'r' have some overlap but as a newcomer to the language, you are better off trying to speak correctly. Note that although Thais may pronounce their 'r's as 'l's sometimes, even they are aware it is technically wrong and there are sometimes TV programmes for Thais to speak Thai accurately! So start off erring on the side of accuracy and relax when you master the language beyond beginner level.

Châwp réu bplào ká?

ชอบหรือเปล่าคะ

Do you like it (or not)?

66. <u>tâo rai</u> เท่าไหร่

Meaning – how much?

Context – we have already met this word several times…the simplest way to use this word if you are not yet confident in or cannot remember the Thai you need, just pick up or point to the item you want to buy and use this word followed by '<u>krúp</u>' or '<u>ká</u>'. Do remember to add the particle to the end as without it, it sounds rather blunt.

Obviously, the chances are, if you are a beginner, you will not understand the response if it is given in Thai but don't let this put you off – make the effort anyway and differentiate yourself.

67. têe năi ที่ไหน

Meaning – where?

Context – literally, 'têe' means *'place'* and 'năi' means *'which?'* (see later in this chapter) but 'năi' is also used as a shorter version of 'têe năi', as we saw at the start of the chat with a taxi driver scenario earlier.

Example:
Koon pák yòo têe năi ká?

คุณพักอยู่ที่ไหนคะ

Where do you live? (Literally, "you staying where?").

This can be a better way of asking where someone lives if they are in Bangkok because often, people who are working in Bangkok are from some other province in Thailand and if the question uses 'bâan' – *'home'* instead, e.g. "bâan (kǎwng) <u>Maem</u> yòo têe <u>nǎi</u>?" the respondent may respond with the name of that province because they assumed that is what you meant, not where they are staying in Bangkok.

Many people who are in Bangkok, even for the long-term, still consider their home to be their family home in their birth province, not least because their name is registered against that address too. They therefore consider that they are just staying, often in a flat, in Bangkok just for work. So, for example, on public holidays, they may say they are going to '<u>glàp</u> bâan' (dtàang <u>jang</u> <u>wàt</u>)' *'go back home (in another province)'* by which they mean their family home. Indeed, this is what most people do and that is why the roads are even more congested than usual when there is a long weekend or on the first and last day of Song-kran etc.

68. <u>tam</u>-<u>mai</u> ทำไม

Meaning – why?

Context – at the beginning of negative questions and the end of positive ones.

Example:
<u>Tam</u>-<u>mai</u> maa cháa jung?

ทำไมมาช้าจัง

Why are you so late?

<u>Bpai</u> <u>Sĭng</u>-<u>ká</u>-bpohr <u>tam</u>-<u>mai</u> <u>krúp</u>?

ไปสิงค์โปร์ทำไมครับ

Why did you go to Singapore?

69. yang ngai ยังไง

Meaning – how?

Context – one usage of this was discussed back in word 23.

Example:

Person A: <u>Bpai</u> <u>yang</u> <u>ngai</u> dee? Person B: <u>Bpai</u> <u>rót</u> <u>fai</u> fáa dee gwàa.

คนแรก: ไปยังไงดี คนที่สอง: ไปรถไฟฟ้าดีกว่า

Person A: How shall we go? / How are we going to get there? Person B: Better to go by skytrain.

Notice the economy of speech in the Thai above, which is a very good thing for beginners trying to talk in Thai!

70. mêua rài เมื่อไหร่

Meaning – when?

Context – one tricky thing to get used to in Thai is to hear or ask this question without any indicator of the tense that it applies to. In reality this is hardly ever an issue because it is obvious from the context already.

Example:
Maa tĕung mêua rài?

มาถึงเมื่อไหร่

When are you arriving? (future tense if 'jà' is added in front) / When did you arrive? (past tense, depending on context).

71. <u>krai</u> ใคร

Meaning – who?

Context – assuming you are in a group of Thais and they are speaking both Thai and English, this and all the other question words are especially useful because you can use them in a single word interjection and demonstrate you can speak a little Thai.

Example:

<u>Káo</u> <u>bpen</u> <u>krai</u> <u>ká</u>?

เขาเป็นใครคะ

Who is that (if both looking at the same person in the distance) / he / she?

72. gèe กี่

Meaning – how many?

Context – as well as the obvious usages such as the ones in the examples below, this word is also used for time: *"how many hours is it"* literally.

Example:

Gèe mohng (láeo) <u>krúp</u>?

กี่โมง (แล้ว) ครับ

What time is it (already)?

As I mentioned in the Preface, telling the time is one of the many areas that differentiate this book from a 'basic' Thai book, which, on my hierarchy is one level above the level of this book. The Thai system of telling time can be a little tricky with a few variations and, as with many other topics, I believe you are very unlikely to be wanting or needing to say the time in Thai. If you do however want to go further, check out the notes at the back of the book for some tips.

Bpai gun gèe kon ká?

ไปกันกี่คนคะ

How many of us are going? / How many in our group (that are going)?

(Rao) sàng gèe yàang láeo?

(เรา) สั่งกี่อย่างแล้ว

How many dishes / items have we ordered already?

73. <u>a</u>-<u>rai</u> อะไร

Meaning – what?

Context – a simple word to learn.

Example:

<u>Kíd</u> <u>a</u>-<u>rai</u> yòo <u>krúp</u>?

คิดอะไรอยู่ครับ

What are you thinking?

Note that you can swap the verb *'to think'*, above, with many of the verbs we have covered already and get a whole set of questions that you can practice and use in real life to easily expand your range e.g. *"what are you doing? / eating?"* etc.

<u>A-rai</u> <u>ná</u> <u>ká?</u>

อะไรนะคะ

Sorry? / Excuse me? / Pardon?

Tips / in my experience / insight: *I need to highlight a point about '<u>a-rai</u> <u>ná</u>' as it is so commonly heard and used. Please do NOT be lazy and pronounce the '<u>ná</u>' in a mid-tone and make it worse by leaving out the '<u>ká</u>' or '<u>krúp</u>'. Over the years, I have heard many foreigners pick this word up quickly but not bother to say it properly and quite frankly, it sounds a bit rude to just blurt out "araina" (not bothering with the tone and rolling both words together) to people who you do not know well enough to be familiar and casual.*

Politeness and pronunciation accuracy should be equal priority to just quantity of words spoken; try to listen carefully to Thai you hear.

74. ...nǎi? ...ไหน

Meaning – which...?

Context – this word can be added after a noun or classifier (word to refer to a set of a particular noun, such as *'loaves'*) to ask which one the person is referring to.

Example:
Person A: <u>Ao</u> dtua <u>nán</u> <u>kà</u>. Person B: Dtua <u>nǎi</u> <u>ká</u>? <u>Un</u> née rěuh <u>ká</u>?

คนแรก: เอาตัวนั้นค่ะ คนที่สอง: ตัวไหนคะ อันนี้เหรอคะ

Person A: Can I get that dress (or any item of clothing; 'dtua' is the classifier). Person B: Which one? Is it this one?

PUTTING IT ALL TOGETHER: SUMMARY OF CHAPTER 5 + 6

This breakout chapter is a summary of Chapters 5 and 6, which were on food words and question words.

Let's focus on a conversation at a restaurant, ordering food and getting the bill and so on. Within it, I'll try and bring in a few questions as well.

Scenario: Eating at a streetside small restaurant (for example, at a typical 'aa-hăan dtaam <u>sàng</u>' – 'food made to order' place.

Tips / in my experience / insight: *it can be a little daunting to some to order food at the roadside stalls and small one-man independent restaurants that are spread all over Thailand. This is usually because the menus and mobile food stall name (describing what particular food the stall sells) are almost* *always in Thai. I urge you to not be like I was when I could not speak (or read) Thai and just go to the mall.*

Most foreigners (unlike me) just go ahead and ask (in English and with however much Thai they know) what the vendor is selling or just point and so on. Yes, it might be awkward and more effort but you will be rewarded with not only some of the best (and cheapest) food in Thailand but also have a chance to interact with 'real' Thai people and maybe even pick up a word or two. I guarantee you that more often than not, you will be very glad you chose to eat like this rather than avoid real Thai life and sit in an air-conditioned mall every day.

Generally, you will have stalls that specialize in a particular thing such as 'gǔay dtǐao' – 'noodles' or 'aa-hǎan dtaam sàng' where you can order pretty much any basic Thai dish based on rice or noodles. Obviously, where in doubt, just point; often the place will have photos or just point at someone else's food.

The main point is don't be put off by not being able to speak or read Thai. In line with this, it is highly unlikely that you will have a conversation like below in Thai if you are a beginner so you will have to substitute or respond with English but that is fine!

And so, I have not suggested sentences that you will find too difficult to remember or even want to learn...after all you are on holiday, not to spend your whole time studying Thai. Just give it a go and learn what you can.

And finally, note that, obviously, a Thai person ordering would simply say a couple of words and be understood; the conversation is an imaginary one for your benefit.

Vendor: <u>Ao</u> <u>a-rai</u> dee <u>krúp</u>?

คนขาย: เอาอะไรดีครับ

Vendor: What would you like?

You: Erm…mee <u>a-rai</u> bâang <u>ká</u>?

คุณ: อึม…มีอะไรบ้างคะ

You: Erm…what do you have?

Vendor: Mee <u>tóok</u> yàang, láeo dtàe <u>sàng</u>. <u>Ao</u> kâao jaan diao r~~ěu~~ gŭay dtĭao?

คนขาย: มีทุกอย่าง แล้วแต่สั่ง เอาข้าวจานเดียว หรือ ก๋วยเตี๋ยว

Vendor: We can make whatever you want. Do you want a rice dish or noodles (soup)?

You: Gŭay dtĭao <u>kà</u>.

คุณ: ก๋วยเตี๋ยวค่ะ

You: Noodle soup please.

155

Vendor: <u>Ao</u> <u>gài</u> r<s>ěu</s> mŏo <u>krúp</u>?

คนขาย: เอาไก่หรือหมูครับ

Vendor: Chicken or pork?

You: Mŏo <u>kà</u>.

คุณ: หมูค่ะ

You: Pork please.

Vendor: <u>Sên</u> <u>lék</u> <u>ná</u>.

คนขาย: เส้นเล็กนะ

Vendor: (Rice) noodles, ok...

...as opposed to '<u>sên</u> <u>yài</u>', which is also made from rice but is a sheet like pasta, a bit like lasagne and there is also '<u>sên</u> mèe', which is vermicelli (thin rice noodles) and '<u>bà</u>-mèe', which are egg noodles. Finally, there is also '<u>wóon</u> <u>sên</u>' – *'glass noodles'*, made from mung beans, used for '<u>yam</u>', not 'gŭay dtĭao'.

You: <u>Kà</u>.

คุณ: ค่ะ

You: Yes please.

Vendor: <u>Ao</u> náam <u>a</u>-<u>rai</u> dee?

เอาน้ำอะไรดี

Vendor: What would like to drink?

(Sometimes, in the more basic places, you won't really have a choice of drinks and it will just be water and there may be a large ice cooler with ice cubes in it for self-service.

In other places, you may have a drinks fridge with soft drinks and maybe even beer! Sometimes, the owner is fine for you to just grab yourself a bottle, especially if they are busy cooking! This is just one example of the easy-going lifestyle in Thailand, especially outside Bangkok in the provinces.)

You: Mee Coke <u>mái</u> <u>ká</u>?

มีโค้กไหมคะ

You: Have you got Coke?

Vendor: Mee <u>krúp</u>, <u>nai</u> dtôo-<u>yen</u>. <u>Yìp</u> <u>ao</u> <u>eng</u> dâai leuy.

คนขาย: มีครับ ในตู้เย็น หยิบเอาเองได้เลย

Vendor: Yes, in the fridge. You can go ahead and take one.

Or, if it is not self-service drinks…

Vendor: Mee <u>krúp</u>. Coke <u>nèung</u> kùat <u>ná</u>. <u>Ao</u> náam-<u>kăeng</u> <u>mái</u>?

คนขาย: มีครับ โค้กหนึ่งขวดนะ เอาน้ำแข็งไหม

Vendor: Yes, we do. One bottle of Coke. Do you want ice?

(By the way, as an aside, you will notice people having ice in beer! It **is** a hot country!)

158

You: <u>Ao</u> <u>kà</u>.

คุณ: เอาค่ะ

You: Yes please

Vendor: Cheuhn <u>nâng</u> <u>krúp</u>.

คนขาย: เชิญนั่งครับ

Vendor: Take a seat.

....and after finishing your food...

You: <u>Gèp</u> <u>dtang</u> dûai <u>ná</u> <u>ká</u>.

คุณ: เก็บตังค์ด้วยนะคะ

You: Can I pay please.

You: ...<u>A-ròi</u> <u>ná</u> <u>ká</u>.

คุณ: ...อร่อยนะคะ

You: ...The food was good.

Worth saying to build goodwill.

Vendor: Kàwp <u>koon</u> <u>krúp</u>. Maa èeg <u>ná</u>.

คนขาย: ขอบคุณครับ มาอีกนะ

Vendor: Thanks. Come back again, ok.

A brief explanation on paying: basically, you say '<u>gèp</u> <u>dtang</u>' (which literally means *'collect the money please'*) in just about any type of food place apart from *'proper'* and maybe slightly posher restaurants, where it is better to say '<u>chék</u> <u>bin</u>' (from the English *'check bill'*...in Thai, words ending in an 'l' sound convert to ending with an 'n' sound).

It is certainly not a hard and fast rule so you do not have to sit there working out the size and poshness of a restaurant on some sort of imaginary scale! It's just a rule of thumb and in most cases, '<u>gèp</u> <u>dtang</u>' is fine. You can also be more lazy and use the circling gesture you will see in Thailand – look out for it.

7. USEFUL PLACES AND DESTINATIONS

Words covered in this chapter		
rohng raem	โรงแรม	hotel
Baan	บ้าน	house / home
raan aa-haan	ร้านอาหาร	restaurant
ta-le	ทะเล	sea
Gaw	เกาะ	Island
sa-naam bin	สนามบิน	airport
Wat	วัด	temple
dta-laad	ตลาด	market
hawng naam	ห้องน้ำ	toilet

NB: Transliteration above written without tone or other pronunciation marks.

75. rohng raem โรงแรม

Meaning – hotel

Context – in reality, beginners are highly unlikely to be attempting to book a hotel in Thai, not least because one needs to know quite a bit of Thai to answer all the questions at check-in and you would probably book online anyway but still I have given the required opening request in Thai below.

Example:
(Calling the hotel) Rohng raem Dusit Thani <u>ná kà</u>. Kǎw jawng <u>hâwng kà</u>.

โรงแรมดุสิตธานี นะคะ ขอจองห้องค่ะ

Dusit Thani? May I book a room please.

163

76. bâan บ้าน

Meaning – house / home

Context – as mentioned before, in certain contexts, 'bâan' refers to the person's family home outside Bangkok in one of the provinces but in others it refers to their own place.

Example:

G<u>làp</u> bâan láeo <u>ná</u> / gàwn <u>ná</u>.

กลับบ้านแล้วนะ / ก่อนนะ

I'm off home.

Remember I said that Thais don't say goodbye? This is one alternative.

77. ráan aa-hăan ร้านอาหาร

Meaning – store / restaurant

Context – 'ráan' is a generic word for all types of store so, for example, a pharmacy is 'ráan kăai yaa', literally – *'store (that) sells medicine'* and an optician is 'ráan dtàt wâen', literally – *'store (that) cuts glasses / lenses'* and so on.

Example:
Keun née bpai ráan aa-hăan Yî-bpòon mái? Ráan dtrong sèe yâek.

คืนนี้ไปร้านอาหารญี่ปุ่นไหม ร้านตรงสี่แยก

Shall we go to a Japanese restaurant tonight? The one by the intersection.

78. ta-le ทะเล

Meaning – sea

Context – used to mean *'seaside'* in everyday usage. Clearly, this is a commonly used word, with Thais and foreigners, given Thailand's beautiful beaches.

Interestingly, 'ta-le saai' means *'desert'* and literally means *'sea (of) sand'*.

Example:
Yàak bpai tîao ta-le jung leuy!

อยากไปเที่ยวทะเลจังเลย

I really want to go to the seaside.

79. gàw เกาะ

Meaning – island

Context – if there is one thing you can do right in Thailand, please pronounce the word for island properly! This will differentiate you from all the other foreigners who say "koh" You can still pronounce it "koh" with other non-Thais but with a Thai person, say 'gàw'. You will get instant credibility.

Example:

Koon Aen keuy bpai Gàw Sa-mŭi mái ká?

คุณแอนเคยไปเกาะสมุยไหมคะ

Have you ever been Koh Samui Anne?

80. <u>sa</u>-năam <u>bin</u> สนามบิน

Meaning – airport

Context – literally translated, *'field of flight'*. Also, a reminder that the Thai pronunciation of the main airport's name is '<u>Sòo</u>-<u>wan</u>-<u>ná</u>-poom'. Yes, there is an 'i' at the end but remember there are many words in the English language with silent letters.

Example:

<u>Bpai</u> <u>sa</u>-năam <u>bin</u> dùan <u>ná</u> <u>ká</u>!

ไปสนามบินด่วนนะคะ

To the airport. Hurry please!

In this context, the driver will ask "<u>kêun</u> taang dùan <u>ná</u>" to which you can just say "<u>kà</u>"

81. <u>wát</u> วัด

Meaning – temple

Context – it should be obvious to any newcomer to Thailand that Buddhism and the temples around the country are a major aspect of Thai society. It is worth visiting a temple while in Thailand; it is an experience that will provide balance and depth to your (I assume) otherwise hedonistic trip.

Example:

Jawn kuey <u>bpai</u> <u>Wát</u> <u>Prá</u> Gâeo <u>réu</u> <u>yang</u>?

จอห์นเคยไปวัดพระแก้วหรือยัง

Have you been to the Temple of the Emerald Buddha John?

82. <u>dtà</u>-làad ตลาด

Meaning – market

Context – often, some of the best experiences of tourists in Thailand are the sights, sounds and smells in a market. It is well worth going to some of Thailand's markets to get a feel for real life…and I don't mean the Floating Market, which is more for tourists.

Example:
Person A: <u>Prôong</u> née <u>bpai</u> <u>dtà</u>-làad <u>Jà</u>-<u>dtòo</u>-<u>jàk</u> <u>gun</u> <u>mái</u>? Person B: <u>Bpai</u> <u>krúp</u>.

คนแรก: พรุ่งนี้ไปตลาดจตุจักรกันไหม คนที่สอง: ไปครับ

Person A: Shall we go to Chatuchak Market tomorrow? Person B: Sure.

83. <u>hâwng</u> náam ห้องน้ำ

Meaning – toilet

Context – this is probably one of the words that actually is very useful to know even if one has no intention of learning Thai. This is especially because, unlike many other cases where you ask a question in Thai but not understand the answer in Thai, in this case, the Thai person can also point the direction to the toilet.

And, of course, the situation where one might need to use this word could be urgent so it is well worth knowing it!

Example:

Kăw tôht <u>krúp</u>; <u>hâwng</u> náam yòo têe <u>năi</u> / taang <u>năi</u> <u>krúp</u>?

ขอโทษครับ ห้องน้ำอยู่ที่ไหน / ทางไหนครับ

Excuse me, where / which way is the toilet please?

Kăw tôht <u>kà</u>. Mee <u>hâwng</u> náam yòo tăeo née / <u>chún</u> née <u>réu</u> bplào <u>ká</u>?

ขอโทษค่ะ มีห้องน้ำอยู่แถวนี้ / ชั้นนี้หรือเปล่าคะ

Sorry, is there a toilet around here / on this floor?

> **Tips / in my experience / insight:** *'to go' is '<u>kâo</u>', literally 'enter' toilet'. So if you are going to say "I need to go / am going to the toilet", it is "(pŏm) <u>dtâwng</u> / <u>jà</u> <u>kâo</u> <u>hâwng</u> náam." And if it is really a case of 'need to', you might need the word 'dùan' – 'urgently' at the end!*

172

8. NUMBERS

Words covered in this chapter		
soon...	ศูนย์....	zero...
sip-ed	สิบเอ็ด	eleven
yee-sip	ยี่สิบ	twenty
rooi...	ร้อย...	hundred...

NB: *Transliteration above written without tone or other pronunciation marks.*

84. sŏon… ศูนย์….

Meaning – zero…

Context – the Thai number system is actually pretty simple hence, to explain the entire system, I have summarized into four so-called 'words'.

The first 'word' is zero all the way up to 10, then two exceptions to the pattern – 11 and 20 – and then the round numbers from 100 up to 1,000,000.

The numbers up to ten are…

Nèung	หนึ่ง	*One*
Săwng	สอง	*Two*
Săam	สาม	*Three*
Sèe	สี่	*Four*
Hâa	ห้า	*Five*
Hòk	หก	*Six*
Jèd	เจ็ด	*Seven*
Bpàed	แปด	*Eight*
Gâo	เก้า	*Nine*
Sìp	สิบ	*Ten*

85. <u>sìp</u>-<u>èd</u> ສິບເອັດ

Meaning – eleven

Context: the first exception i.e. you do NOT say '<u>sìp</u> <u>nèung</u>' but after this, the pattern starts i.e. '<u>sìp</u> săwng, <u>sìp</u> săam'...until...

86. yêe <u>sìp</u> ຍີ່ສິບ

Meaning – twenty

Context: and this is the second exception; after this the pattern resumes so, it is 'yêe <u>sìp</u>-<u>èd</u>', 'yêe <u>sìp</u> săwng'... 'săam <u>sìp</u>-<u>èd</u>' – '31' – all the way up to '99', which is '<u>gâo</u> <u>sìp</u> <u>gâo</u>'...

87. róoi... ร้อย...

Meaning – hundred...

Context: so hopefully the pattern is obvious but for now, two examples to check you are on the right track...

'158' is 'nèung róoi hâa sìp bpàed' and

'641' is 'hòk róoi sèe sìp-èd' and

'893' is 'bpàed róoi gâo sìp săam'.

This pattern continues until we get to...

Pan

พัน

Thousand

Mèun

หมื่น

Ten thousand

Săen

แสน

Hundred thousand

Láan

ล้าน

Million

A billion is said by saying the Thai for a thousand million.

A few more points on numbers:

Sometimes you may hear "róoi gâo gâo". This is just a shorter way of saying *'199'* (which is a common low price for basic quality shoes or clothes in streetside markets).

You may hear 'yêe sìp...' shortened to just 'yìp...' in colloquial speech for numbers from 21 to 29 e.g. 'yìp jèd' is *'27'*.

Adding 'bpen' before any of the big round numbers is like saying *"in the millions / hundreds"* and so on.

> **Tips / in my experience / insight:** *once you get your Thai sim card and you have a local mobile number, try telling a friend your number in Thai and get them to call you. A good initial challenge on pronunciation to see if you are on the right track.*

PUTTING IT ALL TOGETHER: SUMMARY OF CHAPTER 7 + 8

This breakout chapter will be a brief chapter where I discuss a few disparate points that may help you in areas that I have not covered in any detail.

For now, it is worth reiterating that this book does not cover some areas that a basic coursebook would for the simple reason that this book recognises that as beginners and maybe tourists, you may not want to learn that much Thai on your holiday and without learning enough Thai, even if you managed to get your question out correctly, you would struggle to understand the answer without knowing a whole lot more Thai. Also, sometimes, let's be honest, if you speak very little of the language, in certain situations, it can be counterproductive. One example of this might be at bus or train terminals or trying to arrange transport, especially if you have to try to talk to someone sitting behind a plastic barrier or window and there are people queuing behind you. And that is not to mention the fact that, especially when the information being discussed is so important (destination, time of departure, bus no. etc.), it is unwise to confirm these details in a language to which you are new. So, for these reasons, I have not included conversations on booking a hotel, buying a ticket for a bus to a different province and so on.

Having said all that, here are a few random notes that may be helpful, at least to show you are making an effort.

Following up on Chapter 7, let's cover one more place name – Bangkok!

Groong-têp má-hăa-ná-kawn

Before we get onto the more interesting points about the Thai name for Bangkok, let's

183

just make sure we can pronounce it properly. As a reminder of the transliteration rules set out at the start of the book, remember that the underlines take precedence over anything else in determining if a sound is a short sound. So, note that the 'têp' above is a long sound even though it may look like a short sound because of the one 'e'. Think of the sound like 'tâyp' if that helps. Conversely, 'Groong' is a short sound even though it is spelt with two 'o's. I would encourage you to go back to the start of the book and re-read the chapter on the tone and transliteration rules so that you are clear on how to pronounce the Thai in this book without needing to learn to read. It is very important to pronounce Thai correctly as it is a tonal language so pls do put in that bit of effort, which I hope I have kept to an acceptable low level required, compared to other books.

The interesting point about 'Groong-têp Má-hǎa-ná-kawn' is it is actually an abbreviation of a very, very, very long official name. Indeed it is, by far, the longest name for a city in the world! Google it; it is a splendidly rich and verbose statement of what the capital of Thailand represents.

And even 'Groong-têp má-hǎa-ná-kawn' is abbreviated further; in everyday usage, people shorten it to 'Groong-têp'.

Now, let's change tack completely and go back to travelling within Thailand that I mentioned in the opening comments of this chapter. Let's cover a few points on transport words in Thai.

Even if you do not know all the vocabulary necessary for a conversation on buying a ticket for a bus to Pattaya or Ayutthaya, you should already know how you can begin: '<u>bpai</u>' followed by where you want to go. We have also established the generic word for vehicle is '<u>rót</u>'; those inter-province buses are called '<u>rót</u> tua' (which comes from the English word *'tour'*). And the word for 'ticket' is '<u>dtǔa</u>'. And finally, you know the numbers now so you can understand seat numbers or bay numbers said to you in Thai. For a beginner, just these few little words will help you and also be appreciated by local people that you made an effort to speak Thai; the rest, you can say in English. Generally, the people you will deal with at seaside destinations, bus terminals and other touristy places will speak good English.

Finally, let's switch again and cover a few words based on '<u>jai</u>' – *'heart / mind'*, which plays a big part in Thai life, culture and philosophy. We have already met some '<u>jai</u>'

words up to now. Here are some more that I will leave you to find out for yourself. I encourage you to start a conversation with someone in Thailand and ask them the meaning of these words as most Thai people would be delighted to help you speak and understand their language better.

'sĭa jai'

'jèp jai'

'jing jai'

'greng jai' (this one is one of those absolutely central Thai philosophies that define how Thai people behave and react to others; worth asking a Thai person to explain it).

'jai ráwn'

'jai dtên raeng'

9. FLIRTING AND GETTING PERSONAL

Words covered in this chapter		
geng	เก่ง	clever / smart
naa-ruk	น่ารัก	cute / loveable
jao choo	เจ้าชู้	'player' / 'womaniser' / flirt
law	หล่อ	handsome
suay	สวย	beautiful
hawm	หอม	(sniff) kiss
faen	แฟน	girl / boyfriend

NB: Transliteration above written without tone or other pronunciation marks.

88. gèng เก่ง

Meaning – clever / smart

Context – this is a word that is used as a compliment in numerous contexts, so it could also mean *'efficient'*, (doing something) *'well'* and so on.

Example:

Koon Daen gèng jung. Mee faen réu yang ká?

คุณแดนเก่งจัง มีแฟนหรือยังคะ

You're so smart Dan. Have you got a girlfriend?

Notice that it is unnecessary to use the *'you'* pronoun in the Thai version as it is obvious to whom the question is being directed.

Tips / in my experience / insight: *even though Thai culture is conservative, a sense of innocence and playfulness is also integral to 'Thai-ness'. So, in the right context, this kind of rather direct question would not be unusual whereas it would be almost unthinkable in, for example, a British or even Thai to Thai setting.*

One somewhat boring response to this type of innocent flirting or playfulness is to be humble and deny that you are so great e.g. "mâi gèng ràwk krúp". Note that this response sounds more normal in Thai than in English.

Humility is another trait that is integral to Thais. In reality, I am sure you can think of better responses, which should either be funny Thai phrases you have picked up or in many cases, stick to English. It's fine to understand a few words of Thai and reply in English.

If, on the other hand, you are not really a humble person, you can cheekily say 'mee faen yéuh krúp'...which may well be true anyway.

191

89. nâa-<u>rúk</u> น่ารัก

Meaning – cute / loveable

Context – although this word means *'cute'*, it is not necessarily the same sense of cuteness that people mean in the UK, while it actually is somewhat similar to how people use *'cute'* in USA. In Britain (and possibly other countries) *'cute'* is more to do with kids and things somewhat innocent, which is only one of the contexts in which 'nâa-<u>rúk</u>' is used. (Btw, 'kwaam <u>rúk</u>' means *'love'*.)

In Thai this word literally means *'worth loving'* and it is used in a wider range of situations than in English e.g. where you may comment on a scene that is heartwarming or lovely or romantic or sweet, for example.

The other main usage is when talking about the opposite sex...or indeed, the same sex! 'Nâa-rúk' is used as a less forward and subtler (i.e. better!) way of saying someone is attractive in some way, either because of their looks or because of their actions or words etc. In that way, it is similar to how Americans use *'cute'*.

Example:

Ploy nâa-rúk mâak ná krúp.

พลอยน่ารักมากนะครับ

You're so lovely Ploy.

You do not need to say *'you'* in Thai when you address someone by their name. See?

90. j<u>âo</u> chóo เจ้าชู้

Meaning – 'player' / womanizer / flirt

Context – I could probably write an entire chapter on 'j<u>âo</u> chóo' but instead I will do the opposite and keep it brief. This is mainly because those who come across this word in their encounters in Thailand will understand the context, tone and subtleties of the word when they are in that situation in real life. And it is better to find out that way.

What I will say for now, which may not be so obvious, if, as a man, you are called 'j<u>âo</u>-chóo', don't assume it is an insult. The tone is sometimes more mock outrage or teasing.

91. làw หล่อ

Meaning – handsome

Context – the main point with this word is to pronounce it correctly! Do NOT say it as the English word 'law' in an English accent. Go back to the chapter on transliteration and re-read. It is a low tone so say it in a low tone.

Example:

Pôo chaai làw <u>mâi</u> yàak dâai <u>bpen</u> faen. <u>Práw</u> wâa <u>jà jâo</u> chóo!

ผู้ชายหล่อไม่อยากได้เป็นแฟน เพราะว่าจะเจ้าชู้

I don't want a good-looking boyfriend cos he's bound to be a player!

92. sǔay สวย

Meaning – beautiful

Context – the point about mispronuncing the previous word goes double for this word and there are two reasons why. First, this is probably one of the most attempted words by newcomers, especially men (obviously).

Second, mispronouncing it, as with many Thai words, does not just mean that you said it with a lack of clarity (as would be the case in English) but it often means you have said a completely different word. And in this case, mispronouncing 'sǔay' in the most likely way i.e. without bothering to enunciate the rising tone and defaulting to the standard mid tone that you speak English in, means you are actually saying *'unlucky'* or *'cursed'*. And that is not a good thing in a highly superstitious and spiritual country such as Thailand!

Example:

<u>Koon</u> sŭay mâak <u>krúp</u>.

คุณสวยมากครับ

You are really pretty.

> **Tips / in my experience / insight:** *as I mentioned before, rather than 'sŭay', use 'nâa-rúk' for flirting. It's less full on for a first approach in a conservative country and culture. Generally speaking, you're better off erring on the side of more innocent flirting but then again, if you are young and attractive, you can probably pull easily so why be coy!*

93. hăwm หอม

Meaning – (sniff) kiss

Context – a word that definitely needs some explanation as this type of 'kiss' does not really exist in most other countries (I believe). Kissing, whether we mean a peck on the cheek or full on tongues, is called 'jòop'.

'Hăwm' however is a more innocent and cute way of showing affection in Thailand where you lightly *'smell'* the other person's cheek (or, in theory at least, any other part of their body but it is usually cheek). Indeed, the word 'hăwm' means the adjective *'good smell'* and can be used as a verb to smell too. So think of it like a sniff.

Thailand is a conservative country based on a traditional conservative culture (despite impressions you may get from tourist experiences in Bangkok) and that explains why this more inoffensive and subtle way of showing affection exists to this day. You will notice that Thai people rarely show any physical signs of affection toward each other in public so it should be obvious that the so-called French kiss is really something reserved for private moments and when two people are in a committed relationship whereas a 'hǎwm' is something to attempt after a few dates if there is chemistry. Btw, *'I love you'* is 'p̌ǒm / chún rúk koon'.

Having said all that, it is also true to say that Thailand, especially the younger generation, is more open to foreign and Western culture and social norms than maybe fifty years ago when it may have been 'hǎwm', a bit of holding hands and not much more until marriage! However, even then, most younger Thai people still maintain a sense of respectability in society and deep down, still hold traditional values as that is how they have been raised.

You can use 'hăwm' for food that smells good (i.e. simply saying the word as a comment on the great smells of food cooking) or indeed for your partner whose perfume smells good (e.g. 'hăwm jung!').

Example:

Kăw hăwm nòi ná krúp.

ขอหอมหน่อยนะครับ

Can I (sniff) kiss you.

The word 'nòi' is a softener and you will hear it used by Thais e.g. 'maa doo nòi'.

Hăwm gâem dâai <u>mái</u> <u>krúp</u>?

หอมแก้มได้ไหมครับ

Can I give you a sniff kiss on the cheek?

Tips / in my experience / insight: *despite my previous comments, use your intuition and common sense. If the sniff kiss is too cute-sy for you or you feel silly attempting it or you think you can skip it and go for a proper kiss, that's up to your judgement and your individual circumstances.*

As for matters beyond the innocent sniff kiss, I will leave it to your skills and judgement. Just be aware, no matter how confident (sexually or otherwise) your Thai girlfriend (or boyfriend) is, they are still Thai and they hold religious and cultural beliefs that are conservative and they've been raised as such so best not to try to kiss passionately outdoors.

94. faen แฟน

Meaning – girl / boyfriend

Context – this is a generic word for girl-friend, boyfriend, partner and can even be used to refer to your husband or wife. It is also the word for *'fan'* in English and I guess your partner in life is your biggest fan so it makes sense!

Example:

Rao bpen faen gun réu bplào ká?

เราเป็นแฟนกันหรือเปล่าคะ

Are we a couple now (or what)?

Good luck to you if you get this!

Tips / in my experience / insight: *a closing note on this chapter – you may have noticed that I have kept this chapter relatively brief and the example sentences to a minimum.*

The reason for this is that first, it would not be appropriate for this book to include lots of sentences on romantic and sexual topics and second, even if I did, it is unlikely you would use them 'in the heat of the moment' while third, part of the fun of a relationship with someone who speaks a different language is the opportunity to learn each other's language and bond through these experiences.

Some of the best experiences I had were when I first went to Thailand and those initial interactions and friendships I formed. And part of this was definitely my attempts, sometimes successful and sometimes not so successful, at understanding Thai first-hand.

10. EXCLAMATIONS AND (MILD) SWEAR WORDS

Words covered in this chapter		
jing (jing)	จริง (จริง)	really / true
soot yawt	สุดยอด	wow / fantastic
yiam	เยี่ยม	excellent
a-rai wa	อะไรว่ะ	what the hell? / huh? / what??
too-ret	ทุเรศ	approx.. disgusting
baa	บ้า	crazy

NB: Transliteration above written without tone or other pronunciation marks.

Tips / in my experience / insight: *an opening note on this chapter – as a newcomer to Thailand, it can be difficult to build up the courage to speak in a language that is so different to English. Part of the reason for this, as I have said several times in this book, is that even if you have managed to memorise a certain phrase or sentence, there is every chance you will not understand the response if the Thai person assumes you can understand Thai. So, you can be limited to random, short words and phrases.*

This chapter covers some words that foreigners often pick up sooner than 'proper' words. More important, it gives you the context in which to use them.

Unlike other books, I do not believe in shielding you from these words in an attempt to indirectly steer you to speak in a textbook style because I know from personal experience that when you do not know a language, the more exclamatory type of single words are the most fun to learn and also offer a route into a conversation or raise an opportunity to ask questions.

And furthermore, I believe that by giving you some of these words, at least I can explain what they mean to you so that you are better informed and less likely to cause offence compared to the many foreigners I have heard use Thai exclamations both incorrectly and mispronounced. Not only do they sound silly but they often cause offence, so rather than decide in a patronizing way what you should be allowed to learn and what not, you are better off learning to say them properly. You are going to hear these words and you are an adult (I assume) so at least get it right when you do decide to say them.

95. jing (jing) จริง (จริง)

Meaning – really / true

Context – you are almost guaranteed to hear this word if you have stayed even a few days in Thailand. It is definitely a word to try out yourself in Thailand because it allows you to interject in a conversation in a funny way. 'Jing jing!' is like *Honestly!*

Example:
Person A: Jing rěuh? Person B: Jing krúp / Jing jing.

คนแรก: จริงเหรอ คนที่สอง: จริงครับ

Person A: Really? Person B: Yes, really.

96. <u>sòot</u> yâwt! สุดยอด

Meaning – wow / fantastic

Context – a generic exclamation for anything that is amazing or fantastic or simply the best! It can be used (and you may even hear Thai people using it) in mid-sentence in less exclamatory tones to describe something that was so unbelievable, or daring, or unusual, or just worthy of note. Well worth exclaiming this word when you're particularly impressed by something.

To give you further context, '<u>jòot</u> <u>sòot</u> yâwt' means *'orgasm'*, which should make sense – '<u>jòot</u>' means *'point'*. I'll let you connect the dots for yourself.

97. yîam เยี่ยม

Meaning – excellent

Context – a very similar word to the previous one but maybe slightly less exclamatory so can be used pretty similarly to 'excellent' or 'fantastic'.

Example:

Person A: K~eu~n née <u>bpai</u> <u>dtên</u> <u>gun</u> <u>mái</u>?
Person B: Yîam leuy. <u>Bpai, bpai</u>.

คนแรก: คืนนี้ไปเต้นกันไหม คนที่สอง: เยี่ยมเลย ไปไป

Person A: Want to go out clubbing tonight?
Person B: Yeah, sounds great. Let's go.

98. <u>a</u>-<u>rai</u> <u>wá</u> อะไรวะ

Meaning – what the hell? / huh? / what??

Context – it should be obvious that this word can cause offence so pls do NOT start copying this word as soon as you hear it in Thailand as some foreigners do, thinking they are being funny but not realizing they are merely being tolerated as 'a foreigner who does not understand'. Thais use this word in the right circumstances whereas you are more likely to cause offence.

First, note that (as you may have already heard on your stay in Thailand), the standard, more polite way of saying *'excuse me'* or *'what?'* is '<u>a</u>-<u>rai</u> <u>ná</u>?'. So before you even consider saying 'a-rai wá', check whether you mean simply 'a-rai ná krúp / ká?' because you just mean you did not understand something and meant to say *'what?'*.

Second, if you do want to retort using 'a-rai wá', you are safer doing it when you are commenting rhetorically on something that is happening, as opposed to directing this word to someone, which is a big no-no. Do not do that unless of course you know that person well and also your tone does not bear any malice or nastiness but bears more like total confusion or bemusement. So, for example, if you are speaking to your Thai friend and they have said something that sounds like total rubbish or have mumbled something that does not make any sense, 'a-rai wá' is fine as a retort, especially if it is done with a smile and in a funny tone.

Third, note another point about this word, which is that it has variations in pronunciation. Instead of a short, blunt, high tone 'wá', you can say 'waa', which is a longer, softer pronunciation with a very slight high tone. Indeed, you can think of it like a spectrum where at one end is the most abrupt form of the word while, at the other end is a softer, more elongated and more bemused sound and variations in between. So, you can soften your retort slightly by softening your tone slightly and lengthening to 'wáa'. Listen out for these kinds of retorts and expressions that Thais use amongst themselves. You will probably send your friends into hysterics if you manage to blurt out one of these retorts accurately and that is often a great way to break the ice and cross the culture barrier. But like I said earlier, be careful not to cause offence.

99. <u>too</u>-rêt ทุเรศ

Meaning – approximately 'disgusting!'

Context – although this word does not directly translate as *'disgusting!'*, it is pretty close to that kind of an exclamation. It is used (by women) when someone is doing something outrageous or disgusting. In speech it is usually pronounced '<u>too</u>-lêt'.

Example:

<u>Too</u>-rêt! <u>Tam</u> bpai dâai <u>yang</u> <u>ngai</u>?

ทุเรศทำไปได้ยังไง

Unbelievable! How can / could he / you do that?

For example, if you crack one off in public!

100. bâa! บ้า

Meaning – crazy!

Context – you are bound to hear this in Thailand, especially if you are male and sampling some tourist oriented nightlife.

Example:

Fa-ràng bâa! (often pronounced 'Fa-làng')

ฝรั่งบ้า

Crazy foreigner!

For those of you who do not know 'fa-ràng', it is a colloquial Thai word for a Caucasian foreigner (as well as the Thai for *'guava!'*). Usually not meant derogatorily so don't take offence if referred to as such.

'Bâa' might be a mock outraged gentle put-down by a waitress to a customer who is getting a bit too touchy-feely or says something a little too suggestive. Just as with 'a-rai wá', the intended meaning of 'bâa' sits on a spectrum all the way from *"you're so incorrigible"* to *"that's crazy!"* to *"you crazy son-of-a-bitch"*, depending on context.

Bâa réu bplào.

บ้าหรือเปล่า

Are you crazy!

Jà bâa dtaai.

จะบ้าตาย

I'm going to die from going mad

(is the literal translation but the sentiment is more like *"for God's sake!"* or *"This is driving me crazy!"*).

216

And on that happy note we are done with the 100 Thai words to start speaking Thai. :)

I hope you have picked up a few words, at least, that will be of use to you on your trip to Thailand. As I mentioned right at the start of the book, you can absolutely go without speaking any Thai at all but it makes all the difference in the world if you make an effort and try a few words here and there. This book will hopefully have helped you to use those words correctly and pronounce them correctly.

And that is the main thing – speak Thai well and speak it correctly, no matter how few words you actually attempt – and you will be rewarded with appreciation and warmth by Thais who are renowned as some of the warmest, most welcoming people in the world. I wish you all the best and hope your next trip turns out to be even more fulfilling than before and you end up loving Thailand as much as I did when I first learnt Thai.

LIST OF 100 WORDS BY ENGLISH WORD AND MEANING

Here is the full list of 100 Thai words listed by their English meaning for easy lookup straight to the right page.

English meaning	Context / As in..	Page
hello		23
politeness particle	always add this to the end	26
thank you		28
never mind / it's ok		29
good / bad		30
yes / no / not true	more like 'that's true / not true'	32
(to be) well / fine	even more common in Thai	36
sorry		37
I / he / she		38
good luck	can be used like "all the best"	42

name		46
a lot / very	as in very good / tasty...	49
person / people	to talk / ask about nationality	52
language	Eng = "language Eng" in Thai	53
car / vehicle		54
age	useful conversation topic in Thai	56
from	as in "where are you from?"	58
word indicating possession	prefix; as in "my... / his..."	59
to go		74
to like		76
to come		77
to be located at / to live	as in "where are you?"	80
to be	as in "I am, he is..."	82
to buy		83
to discount / reduce	useful for friendly bargaining	84
to go out	very useful word	86
to look / watch	as in going to watch a movie	87
to want to / to want		88
to do / make	even more widely used in Thai	90

to eat		91
to have	very important to learn	92
to know		96
to understand		98
to speak / say		99
expensive		102
comfortable / pleasant	an absolutely central concept in Thai and ubiquitous in Thai life	103
fun / enjoyable	ditto for this word; learn these!	104
hot		106
cold		107
kind / nice		108
calm	and again, central to Thainess	109
very happy / delighted		110
big		111
small		112
fast		113
slow		114

COMMON PHRASE QUICK LOOKUP

Here is an index of key phrases that you will probably either hear during your time in Thailand or want to use yourself in order to have a go at speaking Thai...which you should really do even if you would not understand a reply in Thai. It makes all the difference in the world in terms of connecting with Thai people to have a little go at the language.

So, if you only intend to use this book as a phrasebook, that is still better than not trying at all so here are the places in the book where some key phrases are mentioned. Do try to read the context around the word so that you use the word properly and to best effect. Most misunderstandings happen when a tourist memorises a word but uses it in the wrong situation so context is crucial.

I'm full. p125

Going out / on a trip. p34, p63-65, p75, p77-78, p86, p104, p111, p166

How much is it? p83, p139

Can you give me a discount? p85

You're so lovely. p193

You're beautiful. p197

I love you. p199

Really? Yeah, really! p208

What the hell? p211-213

==================

NOTES FOR FURTHER LEARNING

Although this book is targeted at the majority of foreigners to Thailand who have no interest in learning the language to any great depth, hopefully at least a small number of you will have been inspired to do so...as I was after my first business trip to Thailand for only one week. If that is you, here are some tips that will help – I expand on these points in my intermediate level book – **100 Thai words that make you sound Thai**.

1. Do not translate directly from English to Thai and expect it to be correct. As you will have noticed, I have spent a lot of time in this book highlighting the literal meaning of the Thai words versus the actual meaning. So, in many cases, English

is more verbose than Thai needs to be so *"how are you?"* in Thai is just *"be how?"* because the *"you"* is superfluous. You need to learn Thai by immersing yourself in the language, learn it how it is spoken and try to improve to a point where you think in Thai in your head.

One example of the above point is the word "ao", which Thai people will tell you means *"take"* and will vehemently deny means *"want"* as I have stated in this book. In fact, this is almost totally wrong because they are thinking of "ao" literally, not how it translates in English as a native English speaker would actually say it. So "ao kâao mái?" to a Thai means literally *"do you take rice?"* whereas, in English, we would just ask *"do you want some rice?"* Often Thais use '<u>ao</u>' as short for '<u>ao</u> <u>bpai</u>' which DOES mean *'take'* e.g. '<u>ao</u> <u>sì</u>!' which is short for '<u>ao</u> <u>bpai</u> <u>sì</u>!' i.e. *'take it!'*. See?

Learning any language is learning it for what it is and working out what it means in your own language, which may not be the literal translation so don't try to learn Thai by literally translating every English word in your head in the English order. Ok?

2. The best way, in my opinion, to learn Thai, especially in the early stages of learning, is self-study. It can be tempting to engage a teacher but, in my opinion, this often ends up being a waste of time and money. You are

not yet immersed in the language and you are not invested enough to absorb strange sounding words and ultimately, everything will go in one ear and out the other. Do you agree?

The best way is to study and test out what you have learnt with Thai friends and acquaintances or maybe more commonly, taxi drivers. This kind of brute force style of iterative learning is required to fully absorb the tricky pronunciation and grammar concepts of a language that shares no similarities with English, unlike learning French or German. Most books will have a section near the beginning on pronunciation and mapping of Thai sounds to English as well as the transliteration method. It is critical to spend considerable time on this chapter to get the sounds right because trying to learn the Thai script from the start will only increase the pressure and difficulty and may end up being counterproductive and put you off from labouring with Thai any further.

3. To get up to a level where you can speak Thai comfortably in most everyday situations, you need to use the method in point 2 with this book, move onto **James Higbie's Essential Thai** (basic level). If you get through these two books cover to cover, you will be amazed at your Thai. Then, engage an online Thai teacher if you want and/or check out my intermediate level book. Good luck!

IF YOU'RE GOING TO 'WÂAI', DO IT PROPERLY!

And finally, a cultural point – don't go around Thailand doing the religious / cultural salute ('wâai') to everyone you meet! Yes, that's right, don't do it! At least, to be more precise, don't initiate it.

The 'wâai' is a formal mark of respect when saying *'hello'*, *'goodbye'*, *'thank you'* and sometimes, *'sorry'*, from a younger person to an older person and/or from a person in an 'inferior' social status to a person with higher status (possibly regardless of age) e.g. a sales assistant to a customer, a student to a teacher or professor, or anyone to a monk. You, as a foreign tourist, are normally a customer or guest in most situations i.e. at hotels, in department stores etc. You therefore should NOT 'wâai' first when you enter a shop or leave it. Wait for the staff to 'wâai' you first and then return the gesture if you are keen to do it but a mini head bow and a smile is also sufficient to be polite.

When you 'wâai' staff first, it is not a faux pas on a grand scale and generally it is received well by Thais who are well accustomed to dealing with tourists and they know you mean well and want to show your gratitude and delight at the service you received. But if you want to behave like Thai people, which presumably you do because you are trying to do a Thai gesture of respect, try to restrain yourself from initiating 'wâai''s everywhere you go in Thailand. Notice no Thais ever 'wâai' any staff first but they do 'wâai' each other when they meet and it is usually in a semi-formal setting and initiated by the younger person (but not always) i.e. if two middle-aged couples meet for dinner, they will obviously 'wâai' each other, often at the same time. However, young friends rarely 'wâai' each other because it is a formal gesture not required when you are schoolmates or whatever.

Even more important, if you are going to attempt the 'wâai', at least get it right! The 'wâai' is NOT the same as the Indian gesture so DON'T flare out your elbows like you are about to enter a martial arts contest. I saw Ed Byrne doing this in a BBC documentary on Thailand and I still cringe at the mental image. Not only will you look utterly ridiculous doing this, the Indian / karate salute has the hands too low and could even be seen as disrespectful by Thais.

A proper 'wâai' has the elbows more in than the karate gesture and the height of the hands depends on how much respect is required. A 'wâai' (returned, not initiated) to someone younger or in a 'lower' situational or social status such as a handyman, a sales assistant, a tour guide and pretty much most people you will meet on your trip should be with your hands in front of your chest, your fingertips together and roughly at your chin or lower lip. And your head bow should be just a mini bow.

A 'wâai' to your girlfriend's parents (where you should definitely be the one initiating it) should be with your fingertips in front of your nose and the head bow should be slightly deeper / longer and more respectful.

A 'wâai' to a monk should have the fingertips reaching your forehead, pointing slightly diagonally away and up from your forehead and you should bow your head for longer and show even more respect and humility.

FURTHER INFORMATION

While I do not claim to be and have no desire to be a Thai teacher, I am more than happy to offer advice or answer questions on Thai. I am also happy to help you with your Thai as a conversation partner i.e. in the style of this book and not as a teacher. If you do have any queries, you can contact me on 100thaiwords@gmail.com.

As well as the above, I could suggest Thai teachers for those of you who do want to receive more structured instruction but do bear in mind that it will be the few Thai teachers I am aware of or know in person and not based on some sort of review of all Thai teachers in Thailand.

Finally, I am a bit of a Luddite and so do not have a Facebook site but maybe soon…